LEAP

Five High-Impact
PRACTICES

★ ★ ★ ★ ★ ★ ★ ★ ★ ★ ★ ★ ★ ★

RESEARCH ON LEARNING OUTCOMES, COMPLETION, AND QUALITY

BY JAYNE E. BROWNELL AND LYNN E. SWANER
WITH A FOREWORD BY GEORGE D. KUH

Association
of American
Colleges and
Universities

Association
of American
Colleges and
Universities

1818 R Street, NW, Washington, DC 20009

Copyright © 2010 by the Association of American Colleges and Universities.
All rights reserved.

ISBN 978-0-982-7850-0-3

To order additional copies of this publication or to learn about other AAC&U publications,
visit www.aacu.org, e-mail pub_desk@aacu.org, or call 202.387.3760.

Mixed Sources

Product group from well-managed
forests and other controlled sources
www.fsc.org Cert no. BV-COC-961849
© 1996 Forest Stewardship Council

Contents

★ ★ ★ ★ ★ ★ ★ ★ ★ ★ ★ ★ ★ ★ ★

Foreword

High-Impact Practices
RETROSPECTIVE AND PROSPECTIVE

GEORGE D. KUH

CHANCELLOR'S PROFESSOR OF HIGHER EDUCATION AT INDIANA UNIVERSITY BLOOMINGTON,
AND DIRECTOR, INDIANA UNIVERSITY CENTER FOR POSTSECONDARY RESEARCH

SINCE THE APPEARANCE OF MY 2008 Association of American Colleges and Universities (AAC&U) monograph, *High-Impact Educational Practices: What They Are, Who Has Access to Them, and Why They Matter*, it's been gratifying to see the growing interest expressed by administrators, faculty, and staff in learning more about high-impact practices. In part, this animated groundswell—evidenced by attendance at sessions related to this topic at national and regional meetings and institutional workshops—prompted AAC&U to ask Jayne Brownell and Lynn Swaner to delve more deeply into the research that supports the general pattern of findings associated with the ten high-impact practices identified in the 2007 AAC&U Liberal Education and America's Promise (LEAP) report, *College Learning for the New Global Century*. The fruit of their labor—this monograph—furthers our understanding of and appreciation for the potential of such practices to enhance the learning and personal development of all students, especially those from historically underrepresented groups and those who appear, by traditional measures of precollege achievement, to be underprepared for college-level work. One of the keys to meeting this challenge successfully is determining what works in engaging students more meaningfully in college-level learning.

Over the past decade, I've had many occasions to talk with higher education and popular media writers about this and related topics. The questions most often asked of me relate in one way or another to the things a college could do to boost student engagement. After a time, I began bouncing the question back to the interviewers, asking them to tell me what really made a difference for them in terms of their own learning and personal development. Almost to a person, their answers were tied in some way to writing for their institution's student newspaper or literary magazine or some other venue that gave them a space to practice, apply, and showcase their composition skills.

As these anecdotes began to pile up, I got to thinking about the parallels with some of my own undergraduate experiences. For a time I was the so-called "anonymous" author of the "Headless Norseman" column for the Luther College student newspaper, *CHIPS*. While I spent a lot of time (not always efficiently) preparing my writing assignments—especially for my major field coursework in English and history—I almost always got into the flow when conceptualizing, researching, and writing the Headless column. In fact, one of the undergraduate artifacts of which I am most proud is my *CHIPS* Valentine's Day column; other than my senior project paper, my recollection is that I spent as much time on that column as on other papers I wrote during those years. Although my college newspaper does not compare favorably in terms of advertising revenues or distribution numbers to the Harvard *Crimson* or the Stanford *Daily*, my consternation nevertheless peaked when the *CHIPS* editor in chief cut about a third of my sterling prose because of space limitations!

What is it about my experiences, and those of dozens of national and regional reporters, that makes them stand out so that we readily recall and describe them as especially memorable and important to our lives, then and now? For starters, these activities demanded high-quality work under pressure in real time, in a congenial setting where feedback was plentiful, typically challenging, and often overheard by others. Equally important, the quality of the product was judged by others (often peers) before appearing, and was later evaluated by public opinion. Moreover, producing the material required a dedicated investment of time and energy—at least as much, and by some accounts much more, than was either demanded by or devoted to academic assignments. In other words, what my reporter-colleagues were describing and what I experienced myself is what today we are calling a high-impact activity—an investment of time and energy over an extended period that has unusually positive effects on student engagement in educationally purposeful behavior.

The idea that some programs and practices confer such positive benefits on students in terms of their overall engagement and self-reported outcomes emerged during an in-depth analysis of the relationships between several of the items that are included in the Enriching Educational Experiences benchmark from the National Survey of Student Engagement (NSSE). We found early on, for example, not only that participation in one of these programs—a learning community—was related to higher levels of engagement in the first college year, but also that this elevated level of effort persisted through the senior year (Zhao and Kuh 2004). The more we probed into other programs and practices, the clearer this positive picture became, including strong links to NSSE self-reported gains—the skills students feel they have gained from attending college, including analytical reasoning and writing. Some of these self-reported gains from NSSE are proxies for some of the LEAP Essential Learning Outcomes (see page ix). LEAP is AAC&U's national initiative that champions the importance of a twenty-first-century liberal education—for individual students and for a nation dependent on economic creativity and democratic vitality, and the essential learning outcomes, first described in the LEAP report (2007), provide a framework to guide students' cumulative progress through college. After more

Chart A

The Essential Learning Outcomes

Beginning in school, and continuing at successively higher levels across their college studies, students should prepare for twenty-first-century challenges by gaining:

★ KNOWLEDGE OF HUMAN CULTURES AND THE PHYSICAL AND NATURAL WORLD

> ➤ Through study in the sciences and mathematics, social sciences, humanities, histories, languages, and the arts

Focused by engagement with big questions, both contemporary and enduring

---

★ INTELLECTUAL AND PRACTICAL SKILLS, INCLUDING

> ➤ Inquiry and analysis
> ➤ Critical and creative thinking
> ➤ Written and oral communication
> ➤ Quantitative literacy
> ➤ Information literacy
> ➤ Teamwork and problem solving

Practiced extensively, across the curriculum, in the context of progressively more challenging problems, projects, and standards for performance

---

★ PERSONAL AND SOCIAL RESPONSIBILITY, INCLUDING

> ➤ Civic knowledge and engagement—local and global
> ➤ Intercultural knowledge and competence
> ➤ Ethical reasoning and action
> ➤ Foundations and skills for lifelong learning

Anchored through active involvement with diverse communities and real-world challenges

---

★ INTEGRATIVE AND APPLIED LEARNING, INCLUDING

> ➤ Synthesis and advanced accomplishment across general and specialized studies

Demonstrated through the application of knowledge, skills, and responsibilities to new settings and complex problems

---

Note: This listing was developed through a multiyear dialogue with hundreds of colleges and universities about needed goals for student learning; analysis of a long series of recommendations and reports from the business community; and analysis of the accreditation requirements for engineering, business, nursing, and teacher education. The findings are documented in previous publications of the Association of American Colleges and Universities: Greater Expectations: A New Vision for Learning as a Nation Goes to College (2002), Taking Responsibility for Quality of the Baccalaureate Degree (2004), *and* Liberal Education Outcomes: A Preliminary Report on Achievement in College (2005).

extensive examination of the NSSE findings—including several sets of experimental items that allowed us to learn more about service learning, student–faculty research, study abroad, internships, and senior culminating experiences—we were convinced that we were onto something, having discovered some patterns in the data that began to explain how and why participating in such activities was beneficial.

It is reassuring that the conclusions Brownell and Swaner draw from the published research essentially affirm the relationships between the high-impact practices and selected dimensions of student success, persistence, and changes in attitudes and behaviors. As with any literature review, their work represents a snapshot in time—in this instance through 2009. Just in the past year, new findings from the Wabash National Longitudinal Study on Liberal Arts Education show that the good practices in undergraduate education that constitute many of the conditions at the foundation of the high-impact practices have unusually positive effects after controlling for precollege differences (Pascarella, Seifert, and Blaich 2010; Seifert et al. 2010).

THE NEXT FRONTIER

Brownell and Swaner suggest that sewing several high-impact practices into one activity may further magnify the positive impact of the experience. For example, imagine what the student experience would be like if all first-year students at your institution took a small (twenty-five students or fewer) writing- or inquiry-intensive seminar with common readings and a service-learning component. Students would have intellectual experiences in common to discuss as they walk together to and from class, to the residence hall, campus union, or parking lot. Every student would know a faculty member well and have more than a few classmates to study with. Linking this course to one or two others taken by the same students would create the kind of learning community that Brownell and Swaner remind us might well strengthen the social bonds among the students and that, in turn, will enhance their sense of belonging and support—conditions typically associated with higher persistence and satisfaction levels. In fact, some of the institutions participating in the Documenting Effective Educational Practices project, which was profiled in *Student Success in College*, used some of these high-octane approaches, such as the First-Year Seminar at Wheaton College, the Common Intellectual Experience at Ursinus College, and the Entering Student Program at the University of Texas at El Paso (Kuh et al. 2005).

While stitching together two or more high-impact practices would likely enhance their effect, NSSE data suggest that participating in any one high-impact activity can boost engagement and even yield compensatory benefits to students who most need the help, such as those from historically underrepresented groups and those who are less well-prepared for college (Kuh 2008). The Wabash National Longitudinal Study of Liberal Arts Education reports similar results (Pascarella, Seifert, and Blaich 2010; Seifert et al. 2010). To explain in part why these practices work so well, I posited six student behaviors that the ten LEAP high-impact practices induce (Kuh 2008, 14–17):

1. investing time and effort

2. interacting with faculty and peers about substantive matters

3. experiencing diversity

4. responding to more frequent feedback

5. reflecting and integrating learning

6. discovering relevance of learning through real-world applications

It is the combination of these behaviors that make these practices so powerful. And there are other educationally powerful conditions that may well be worthy of the label "high-impact." Recent NSSE (2009) findings related to writing courses and student–faculty research point to two such conditions associated with high levels of engagement and desired outcomes. The first condition is setting appropriate expectations for the activity. In the context, for example, of student–faculty research, this requires clarifying for students what their role will be at various stages in the inquiry process. Those students who are actively involved in determining the objectives of the research and at other points in conducting the research—reviewing the literature, collecting data, writing up the results, presenting the findings in different venues—benefit much more from the experience than those students whose role is limited to collecting data. The second condition is public demonstration of what one can do, as is often expected in a capstone or other form of senior culminating experience. This can take various forms in which students, in a structured way, synthesize and integrate what they have learned and, through the completion and presentation of a project, examination, or set of artifacts accompanied by a self-reflective essay, show what they can do with the information, competencies, and skills they have gained.

It stands to reason that these key conditions can be adapted and incorporated into any teaching and learning situation inside or outside the classroom to promote higher levels of student performance. As I mentioned at the outset, there are doubtless other high-impact activities, in addition to writing for the campus newspaper, in which large numbers of students participate. Some that come to mind are participation in intercollegiate athletics and touring bands, choirs, and other musical and theatrical groups, all of which are accompanied by frequent feedback from "experts" (coaches, directors) that have immediate consequences and that affect the performance of others.

There is a risk, certainly, of assuming certain practices or activities are "high-impact" in the absence of either strong empirical support or a compelling theoretical rationale. And so I join with Brownell and Swaner in urging that more research be done to determine what practices and what aspects of those practices seem either to have the greatest overall impact or are associated with especially robust outcomes. In the meantime, we now know enough to urge faculty and staff to find ways to adapt and sew these and other good liberal arts educational practices into teaching and learning settings, inside and outside the classroom and on and off the campus. In addition to the classroom, lab, or studio, the other venue in which a large majority of students find themselves is the workplace.

CAN WE MAKE EMPLOYMENT A HIGH-IMPACT ACTIVITY?

By one estimate, two-thirds of students at four-year institutions and four-fifths of their counterparts at two-year institutions work during college (Horn and Nevill 2006). Is it possible to structure certain aspects of the employment experience—especially on-campus, but also off-campus employment—so that work enriches, rather than competes with or is orthogonal to, an institution's learning goals for its students? I believe this is doable, if faculty and staff systematically create the conditions characteristic of the high-impact practices identified in the LEAP report. In our most recent analysis of NSSE data, working either on or off campus was found to be positively related to several dimensions of student engagement, especially for full-time students (McCormick, Moore, and Kuh 2010). Unsurprisingly, students who worked on campus generally benefitted more than their counterparts who worked off campus. But contrary to expectations, some of the stronger positive effects on engagement were experienced by full-time students who worked more than twenty hours per week on campus. On balance, the benefits of working during college appear to be mediated by student engagement. This suggests that one potentially productive way to optimize the positive benefits of work and study is to induce students intentionally to connect what they are learning in class with experiences in the work setting. How might this be done?

One approach is to bring together small groups of students who work in the same office or functional area to reflect systematically on and discuss how what they have experienced or learned on the job informs or connects to their studies, presently or in the past. Similarly, students can be encouraged to think about how what they are learning in class and elsewhere informs or is helpful to their job or advances or clarifies their career aspirations. Engaging students in this kind of reflection may be difficult initially, because such connections will not always be immediately apparent—especially to those holding what might be considered less intellectually challenging positions, such as in food service or as office assistants. Indeed, my own experience is that most students will have little to say in the first and even the second meetings. To jump-start the discussion, it can be helpful for an upper-division student who is articulate on these matters to participate. Over the course of several sessions, after hearing some others talk about their experiences, most, if not all, students will likely begin to make connections between their work experiences and their studies. And the more practice students have doing this, the better they will get at these challenging tasks of reflection, integration, and synthesis. Such high-level cognitive skills are best acquired through modeling, practice, feedback, and more practice and feedback. Through such conversations, students may well deepen their understanding of their values and long-term goals—a behavior that is also positively linked to student persistence and other measures of success in college. Equally important, students will have made important strides toward becoming reflective practitioners, a necessary attribute for lifelong learning. Lee Shulman eloquently articulated this long-term benefit of engagement:

> Learning begins with student engagement, which in turn leads to knowledge and understanding. Once someone understands, he or she becomes capable of performance or action. Critical reflection on one's practice and understanding leads to higher-order thinking in the form of a capacity to exercise judgment in the face of uncertainty and to create designs in the presence of constraints and unpredictability. Ultimately, the exercise of judgment makes possible the development of commitment. In commitment, we become capable of professing our understandings and our values, our faith and our love, our skepticism and our doubts, internalizing those attributes and making them integral to our identities. These commitments, in turn, make new engagements possible—and even necessary… [Thus] engagement is not solely a proxy; it can also be an end in itself. Our institutions of higher education are settings where students can encounter a range of people and ideas and human experiences that they have never been exposed to before. Engagement in this sense is not just a proxy for learning but a fundamental purpose of education (Shulman 2002, 38).

Last Word

High-impact practices are developmentally powerful because they combine and concentrate other empirically validated pedagogical approaches into a single multidimensional activity that unfolds over an extended period of time. These practices are at the heart of a liberal education. Equally important, all the evidence so far suggests that they benefit all students. At the same time, while promising, they are not a panacea. Only when they are implemented well and continually evaluated to be sure they are accessible to and reaching all students will we realize their considerable potential.

Preface

About Liberal Education and America's Promise (LEAP):
EXCELLENCE FOR EVERYONE AS A NATION GOES TO COLLEGE

LIBERAL EDUCATION AND AMERICA'S PROMISE (LEAP) is a decade-long national initiative launched by the Association of American Colleges and Universities (AAC&U) in 2005 to align the goals for college learning with the needs of the new global century. Extending the work of AAC&U's Greater Expectations initiative, LEAP seeks to engage the public with core questions about what really matters in college, to give students a compass to guide their learning, and to make the aims and outcomes of a liberal education—broad knowledge, intellectual and practical skills, personal and social responsibility, and integrative learning—the expected framework for excellence at all levels of education. The LEAP initiative is especially concerned with students who, historically, have been underserved in higher education.

LEAP INCLUDES THREE PRIMARY AND CONCURRENT STRANDS OF WORK:

➢ a **research initiative** designed to provide evidence on the essential learning outcomes of a liberal education and periodic reports on progress in helping students meet twenty-first-century educational standards

➢ the **Campus Action Network**, which comprises campuses of every kind from across the country that are working with LEAP to articulate high expectations for liberal education, connect educational practices and assessments to those expectations transparently, and ensure that all their students achieve the essential learning outcomes

➢ a **public advocacy campaign** for liberal education, carried out nationally by the educational, business, community, and policy leaders in the LEAP National Leadership Council and regionally through advocacy initiatives in a set of partner states

---

LEAP addresses the entire college curriculum, including both professional fields and the liberal arts and sciences. The overarching principles that define liberal education changed fundamentally in the early part of the twentieth century, when the academic disciplines displaced the classical "core" curriculum. In the twenty-first century, the principles of liberal education are changing once again.

Contemporary liberal education has expanded to foster the deep learning and the practical skills and experience that all students need. It has become more powerful by bridging the traditional divides between "liberal" and "applied" learning in order to prepare all college students for success in a diverse democracy and an interconnected world.

Through LEAP, AAC&U is working with campuses to accelerate the pace of change and to organize local, regional, and national community and policy dialogues about the educational issues at stake. At a time when so many are seeking a college education, students deserve far better guidance on the kinds of learning that will serve them best in the era ahead. Highly intentional planning, teaching, and assessment to improve learning and sustain all students' engagement are needed to ensure that students achieve the sophisticated outcomes expected from a contemporary liberal education.

This publication is one in a series of publications supported by the LEAP initiative. The major national report published by the LEAP National Leadership Council in 2007, *College Learning for the New Global Century*, issued a call to educators and to the nation about the importance of a set of essential learning outcomes. It argued that we must fulfill the promises of education for all students who aspire to a college education, especially to those for whom college is a route—perhaps the only possible route—to a better future. Based on extensive input from both educators and employers, the recommendations in this report respond to the new global challenges today's students face. It describes the learning contemporary students need from college, and what it will take to help them achieve it.

Another important publication in the LEAP series, written by George D. Kuh, was released in 2008 and called *High-Impact Educational Practice: What They Are, Who Has Access to Them, and Why They Matter*. This publication addresses a set of educational practices identified in the original 2007 LEAP report and discusses the research that demonstrates the impact these practices seem to have on student success. *Five High-Impact Practices* builds on this earlier work and delves even deeper into the research on a small set of selected high-impact educational practices that improve student retention, increase graduation rates, and have potential to enable students to achieve the outcomes they will need in this new global century.

OTHER TITLES FROM LIBERAL EDUCATION AND AMERICA'S PROMISE:

LEAP

FOR MORE INFORMATION ABOUT LEAP AND TO PURCHASE LEAP PUBLICATIONS, VISIT WWW.AACU.ORG/LEAP.

Acknowledgments

★ ★ ★ ★ ★ ★ ★ ★ ★ ★ ★ ★ ★ ★ ★ ★ ★

WE WOULD LIKE TO THANK EVERYONE AT THE ASSOCIATION OF AMERICAN COLLEGES AND UNIVERSITIES (AAC&U) who gave us guidance and feedback on this project, from the original literature review in 2008 through the publication of this monograph, with special thanks to Alma Clayton-Pedersen, former vice president for education and institutional renewal and current senior scholar; Nancy O'Neill, director of programs for the Office of Education and Institutional Renewal; and Debra Humphreys, vice president for communications and public affairs. We also thank Laura Donnelly-Smith and Shelley Johnson Carey for their excellent editing during this project.

OUR THANKS GO TO ERIN MCDOWELL, who acted as a research assistant during the development of the original literature review, and who continued to give her feedback throughout this project.

WE WOULD ALSO LIKE TO THANK LEE KNEFELKAMP, who inspires us through her long-standing commitment to AAC&U and to her students at Teachers College, Columbia University.

JAYNE WOULD LIKE TO RECOGNIZE ALL HER COLLEAGUES AT HOFSTRA UNIVERSITY, especially Sandy Johnson, vice president for student affairs, for their ongoing support of her work with AAC&U.

FINALLY, WE THANK CARNEGIE CORPORATION OF NEW YORK AND LUMINA FOUNDATION FOR EDUCATION for their support of this project and for helping to make this publication possible. The statements made and views expressed are solely the responsibility of the authors.

—Jayne Brownell and Lynn Swaner

Introduction

★ ★ ★ ★ ★ ★ ★ ★ ★ ★ ★ ★ ★ ★ ★ ★

IN THE ASSOCIATION OF AMERICAN COLLEGES AND UNIVERSITIES' 2007 REPORT, *College Learning for the New Global Century,* the National Leadership Council for Liberal Education and America's Promise (LEAP) identified ten innovative, "high-impact" practices that are gaining increased attention in higher education.[1] These practices are thought to lead to higher levels of student performance, learning, and development than traditional classroom experiences, and are often implemented in an effort to meet the unique needs of a new generation of students:

> As higher education has reached out to serve an ever wider and more diverse set
> of students, there has been widespread experimentation to develop more effective
> educational practices and to determine "what works" with today's college students.
> Some of these innovations are so well established that research is already emerging
> about their effectiveness (AAC&U 2007, 5).

In discussing the evidence for the success of these practices, Kuh (2008) asserts that, when done well, they are associated with a range of desirable learning and personal development outcomes, and recommends that all students in higher education participate in at least two high-impact practices, one in their first year and another within their academic major coursework.

Despite the promise of these practices, they are neither widespread in higher education nor part of the average college student's educational experience. As the 2007 LEAP report explains, "these active and engaged forms of learning have served only a fraction of students" (5). This is particularly significant when considering the demographics of such participation: "New research suggests that the benefits are especially significant for students who start farther behind. But often, these students are not the ones actually participating in the high-impact practices" (5). In addition to the question of who participates in these practices and what kinds of benefits

---

1. The high-impact practices indentified in the report are: first-year seminars, common intellectual experiences, learning communities, writing-intensive courses, collaborative projects, undergraduate research, diversity/global learning, service learning, internships, and capstone courses.

there may be for various populations, it is important to consider the quality of these experiences. As Kuh (2008) states, "to engage students at high levels, these practices *must be done well*" (20, italics in original). If high-impact practices have differing effects, we need to know the variability of impact not only across practices, but also between permutations of the same practice.

This monograph examines the existing body of research to explore many of the questions raised with regard to five high-impact practices: first-year seminars, learning communities, service learning, undergraduate research, and capstone experiences. [2] One chapter is devoted to each of these practices, and an additional chapter examines outcomes of educational approaches that combine two or more of the practices. The last chapter summarizes the lessons learned from the review of the five practices. Specifically, throughout this monograph we explore the following questions:

> What are the known outcomes for students who participate in these five practices?

> Are the outcomes the same for traditionally underserved student populations,[3] namely students from historically underrepresented minority groups, students from low-income families, and students who are first in their families to attend college (first-generation students)?

> Are there conditions under which positive outcomes are more likely to be found, and, if so, what design and implementation strategies should practitioners employ to maximize the impact of these practices?

> What are the current strengths and weaknesses of the outcomes literature as a whole, and how can we strengthen our knowledge about these practices?

If we are to create what Leskes and Miller (2006) have called "purposeful pathways" for student learning, practitioners and researchers need a better understanding about the variation among and within these practices, and which variables are likely to lead to the most positive outcomes for our students and our institutions.

---

2. Throughout this review, emphasis has been given to peer-reviewed, published research on outcomes for these high-impact practices, with a preference for studies with multi-institutional samples and sound research practices. For brevity, not every study reviewed is cited in this report.

3. Rather than standardize the various terminologies utilized to describe subgroups of underserved students, this review utilizes the language put forth by the authors of each study or article under review. For example, some of the research reviewed refers to students as African American, while other studies refer to students as black; in each case, the terminology utilized by that particular study or article was utilized in its description.

Components of Successful High-Impact Practices

Within each high-impact practice, our research identified components for success. While not exhaustive, the suggestions below detail some best practices for implementing high-impact activities.

WITHIN FIRST-YEAR SEMINARS

➤ Establish seminar goals before designing a program, and choose the seminar format that fits those goals.

➤ Use instructional teams whenever possible; for example, build a resource team that includes faculty, advisers, librarians, and technology professionals.

➤ Use engaging pedagogies that are active and collaborative in nature, including group work, interactive lectures, experiential learning, and problem-based learning.

➤ Help students see that the skills they need to succeed in the seminar are skills they will use throughout college and after graduation.

WITHIN LEARNING COMMUNITIES

➤ Be intentional in linking courses.

➤ Support students in traditional gateway courses and "weed-out" courses that have high rates of failure.

➤ Consider tying an extended orientation or integrative seminar to the learning community.

➤ Use instructional teams, such as the one described for first-year seminars above.

➤ Invest in faculty development to ensure that courses are fully integrated, with coordinated materials, assignments, out-of-class trips, and grading rubrics.

➤ Use engaging pedagogies.

WITHIN UNDERGRADUATE RESEARCH PROGRAMS

➤ Encourage faculty to provide mentoring, rather than just program oversight, and attend to the quality of the mentoring relationship (balancing challenge with support).

➤ Provide opportunities for "real-life" applications, whether through publication, presentations, or project implementation.

➤ Offer intentionally designed curricula that enhance students' research skills and build those skills over time, including prior to intensive undergraduate research experiences.

WITHIN SERVICE-LEARNING PROGRAMS

➤ Create opportunities for structured reflection.

➤ Ensure that faculty connect classroom material with the service experience.

➤ Require enough service hours to make the experience significant.

➤ Focus on the quality of the service, ensuring that students have direct contact with clients.

➤ Oversee activities at the service site.

Source: Adapted from Brownell and Swaner 2009

CHAPTER 1

First-Year Seminars

★ ★ ★ ★ ★ ★ ★ ★ ★ ★ ★ ★ ★ ★ ★

OF THE FIVE EDUCATIONAL PRACTICES REVIEWED IN THIS MONOGRAPH, first-year seminars have existed for the longest period of time and are the most common on college campuses. Seminars for new students first appeared on college campuses around 1910 and were a common staple for several decades (Gordon 1989). Those early courses were similar in content to most first-year seminars today. They focused on acclimating students to living and learning in a college environment, taught study skills and time management, introduced students to campus resources, and taught students about their institution's policies, history, and traditions. While nine out of ten students were required to take an orientation class in 1938 (Mueller 1961), faculty at that time began to question the academic value of these courses, and they had nearly disappeared from campuses by the mid-1960s.

The resurgence in new-student seminars began in the early 1970s, and by the 1980s the seminars had become common once again. While the exact number of campuses that offer first-year seminars is impossible to determine with certainty, it has been reported that between 85 percent and 95 percent of two-year and four-year campuses offer some type of first-year seminar (Goodman and Pascarella 2006; National Resource Center on the First-Year Experience and Students in Transition 2006; Policy Center on the First Year of College 2002).

Barefoot (1992) developed a typology to classify these seminars, and that typology has been adopted by the National Resource Center for the First-Year Experience and Students in Transition. It identifies five main types of seminars:

1. *Extended orientation seminars:* Often called orientation classes or "University 101" courses, these are the most common type of first-year seminar. They aim to provide information to help students transition to a new environment, similar to the original first-year seminars. These courses may be taught by faculty, staff, or administrators from student affairs, or student peer mentors.

2. *Academic seminars with uniform content across sections:* These courses address the intellectual transition to college more than the personal transition. They may include academic skill-building topics, particularly writing or critical thinking, but within the context of an interdisciplinary or theme-oriented academic course designed for first-year students. These courses are more likely to be taught by faculty, or team-taught with a member of the student affairs staff or a student peer mentor.

3. *Academic seminars with variable content:* These courses are very similar to the academic seminars described above except that they are more likely to be based in a single discipline rather than being interdisciplinary, so content areas will vary from section to section.

4. *Preprofessional or discipline-linked seminars:* Courses in this category are designed to introduce students to a particular discipline or profession and are typically offered by professional schools or specific disciplines.

5. *Basic study skills seminars:* Usually targeted for underprepared students, these courses focus mainly on college-level skill development. They are the least common type of first-year seminar.

Despite the longstanding history of the first-year seminar, research about their effectiveness was very limited until the late 1980s. Goodman and Pascarella (2006) note that when Pascarella and Terenzini wrote the 1991 version of *How College Affects Students*, very there was little research to review. However, by the 2005 version of the book, there were more than forty studies available for review. Still, for this monograph, we found that much of the available research dates from the 1990s, with the pace of published research slowing down after 2000.

Notes on the Research Included in This Review

Before looking at student outcomes, it is worth noting the treatment of two significant collections of first-year seminar outcome studies for the purposes of this review.

The Exploring the Evidence monographs, published by the National Resource Center on the First-Year Experience and Students in Transition, include research summaries about the first-year seminars offered at more than 120 colleges and universities (Barefoot 1993; Barefoot et al.1998; Tobolowsky, Cox, and Wagner 2005). While these reports provide useful information for institutions that are looking to create or improve their own seminar, we viewed them as representing "best practices" for these seminars and did not include them in this review.

Using a very different approach, in the 2005 edition of *How College Affects Students*, Pascarella and Terenzini provide a thorough and concise analysis of the outcomes research related to first-year seminars. This current review does not intend to duplicate that work, but will highlight some of the key studies and findings, and look at research published since that time, as well as pay special attention to what is known about the impact of first-year seminars on underserved student populations.

OUTCOMES OF FIRST-YEAR SEMINARS

Persistence

The consensus in the literature is that first-year seminars have a positive influence on student persistence—particularly retention from freshman year to sophomore year—when compared with persistence rates of students who did not participate in a seminar (e.g., House and Kuchynka 1997; Lang 2007; Miller, Janz, and Chen 2007; Starke, Harth, and Sirianni 2001; Williford, Chapman, and Kahrig 2000-2001).

Fidler and his colleagues have studied the University 101 course at the University of South Carolina since 1973 (e.g., Fidler 1991; Fidler and Goodwin 1994; Fidler and Moore 1996). In one of the most frequently cited articles in the first-year seminar literature, Fidler studied every entering cohort from 1973 to 1988 and compared the sophomore retention rates of seminar participants and nonparticipants (Fidler 1991). While the study controlled for motivation and multiple background demographic and academic characteristics, the two groups were not intentionally matched in any way. In all years studied, first-year seminar participants persisted at higher rates than nonparticipants, and this finding reached significance in eleven of the sixteen years. A greater than 7 percent difference in retention rates was found in multiple years. Further, in most years, seminar participants had lower predicted grade point averages (GPAs) than their peers, but still had higher persistence rates.

One of the few multi-institutional studies of first-year seminars approached the question of persistence from a different angle (Porter and Swing 2006). The goal of this study was to determine what elements of these seminars led to increased likelihood of student persistence. The study looked at students at forty-five four-year colleges and universities, measuring students' intention to persist rather than persistence itself. The authors reviewed literature showing that students' expressed intent to persist is an accurate measure of students' true behavior, and they found that the intended rate of persistence matched the typical persistence rates for the forty-five schools in the study. To ensure that the content, structure, and goals of the courses studied were as similar as possible, extended orientation seminars were the only type included in the study. In addition to controlling for student background characteristics, the authors also controlled for institutional characteristics, such as selectivity, resources, and institutional type (i.e., public, private, doctoral-granting, etc.). The authors found that the two elements most related to students' intention to persist were institutional effectiveness in teaching study skills and educating about health and wellness topics. They note that these are the two areas that faculty often feel the least equipped to address, but they are the most significant to students. They theorize that for health education, it may not be the material covered that is most important to students, but the fact that by discussing health topics, faculty, "are de facto expressing caring about students… [acknowledging] that students are more than 'cognitive beings'" (Porter and Swing 2006, 106).

Graduation Rates

Few studies have followed students through college to examine the influence of first-year seminars on graduation rates. However, those that have followed students have found higher graduation rates for seminar participants at the end of four, five, and six years from entry (Lang 2007; Schnell, Louis, and Doetkott 2003; Starke, Harth, and Sirianni 2001; Williford, Chapman, and Kahrig 2000-2001).

Academic Achievement/Grade Point Average

Findings about student grades are not as clear cut as the results regarding persistence. While many studies have found that first-year seminar participation has a positive effect on first-term and/or first-year grades (Friedman and Alexander 2007; House and Kuchynka 1997; Maisto and Tammi 1991), another did not find any significant differences between the GPAs of seminar participants and nonparticipants (Fidler 1991). Another study found significant differences for seminar participants in the short term, but found the advantages faded after the first year (Lang 2007).

Other Outcomes

Barefoot (2000) has called for campuses to think beyond retention outcomes to focus on student learning. Upcraft, Garder, and Barefoot (2005) also challenge schools to broaden their definition of student success to include developing intellectual and academic competence, building interpersonal relationships, exploring identity, developing career goals, maintaining health and wellness, clarifying values and beliefs, developing multicultural awareness, and developing a sense of civic responsibility. A few recent studies have taken on those challenges. Engberg and Mayhew (2007) examined democratic outcomes, such as commitment to social justice, multicultural awareness, and a propensity toward active and causal thinking, as outcomes of the first-year seminar experience. The authors compared first-year students in an extended orientation seminar with an emphasis on diversity to matched peers taking a first-year communication class or a first-year engineering class. Despite no pretest differences on these measures between any of the groups, the students in the first-year seminar reported significantly more growth in commitment to social justice and multicultural awareness than the other two groups. Both these students and the engineering group showed significant growth in active and causal thinking.

Keup and Barefoot (2005), in one of the few multi-institutional first-year seminar studies, looked at all students who completed both the Cooperative Institutional Research Program survey and the Your First College Year survey in 2001 to compare trends between seminar participants and nonparticipants. They found that first-year seminar students reported that they had more faculty interaction, spoke in class more often, and were less likely to skip class or arrive late. Participants also reported being more likely to develop a network of friends, discuss course content with peers outside of class, study with other students, use campus resources, attend campus events, and participate in volunteer activities.

Other findings in the literature determined that compared to nonparticipants, students in first-year seminars demonstrate:

> More positive relationships with (Fidler 1991; Starke, Harth, and Sirianni 2001) and more informal interactions with faculty (Maisto and Tammi 1991)

> Greater perception of faculty support and care (Sommers 1997)

> Greater knowledge of (Schwitzer, McGovern, and Robbins 1991) and use of campus resources (Fidler 1991; Wilkie and Kuckuck 1989)

> More involvement in campus activities (Starke, Harth, and Sirianni 2001)

> More ability to manage their time (Sommers 1997)

OUTCOMES FOR SPECIFIC STUDENT POPULATIONS

A significant gap in the first-year seminar literature is the lack of attention to the outcomes of seminars for specific student populations. While there is discussion about the impact of seminars based on level of academic preparation, very few studies focus on underserved populations at all, and rarely is this investigation the main purpose of the study. Only one identified article is focused on low-income students; the study it describes looks at a four-year college in which half of the students earn $20,000 per year or less (Anselmo 1997). The first-year seminar studied was designed for the college's Search for Education, Elevation, and Knowledge (SEEK) program, which is made up of the most academically and economically disadvantaged students on campus. The seminar was designed such that students gathered for a reunion in each of the three terms following the course. The hope was that the reunions would help renew and extend the academic and social connections made during the first-year seminar. Compared with the SEEK group that took the seminar without reunions, the first-year seminar reunion participants had significantly higher GPAs, earned more credits, and were more likely to persist over the following three years. However, no comparisons were made with non-SEEK students.

Racial or ethnic factors are usually controlled for early in the analysis of most studies, making it impossible to determine differential impacts for these groups. Some studies simply note that the results did not vary based on race or ethnicity. An exception is the Fidler and Godwin (1994) study, which examined the impact of the University 101 first-year seminar program on African American students at the University of South Carolina. In contrast to national trends, these students achieved higher rates of retention from first year to sophomore year than their white peers for nineteen consecutive years. Further, African American students who participated in the seminar persisted at a greater rate than African American students who did not participate in nine of thirteen years studied.

Wilkie and Kuckuck's 1989 study alone specifically noted an effect of first-year seminars on first-generation students. Most of the students in the study were first generation and academically at risk, with all students predicted to earn GPAs of 1.5 or lower. Students were randomly placed into either a participant or nonparticipant group, and only those who successfully completed the seminar, and therefore the experimental treatment, were included in the analysis. The two groups earned comparable GPAs during their first term, but by the third year, the first-year seminar group's GPAs were significantly higher than those of the control group. Similarly, persistence of students in the participant group surpassed that of their peers over time, and by the third year, the difference approached statistical significance. The seminar group was also more likely to use campus resources than were their nonparticipant peers.

MODERATING VARIABLES

Swing (2002) reported the results of the First-Year Initiative study conducted by the Policy Center on the First Year of College. This benchmarking survey was conducted to determine the types of first-year seminars that exist across the United States as well as the range of student outcomes associated with these seminars. Researchers surveyed both seminar coordinators/directors and more than thirty thousand first-year seminar students. No nonparticipant comparison group was surveyed. Ten learning outcomes were studied, along with course delivery, effectiveness, and students' overall satisfaction with their institutions. The most common seminar type was the transition (extended orientation) seminar, which was also found to be the type that led to the greatest number and range of student outcomes studied. Students rated the seminars as highly effective at improving study strategies, out-of-class engagement, knowledge of academic services, knowledge of wellness issues, connections with faculty, connections with peers, and time management/prioritization. Discipline-based seminars were rated as the least effective type by students, and these seminars were also rated the lowest by students at utilizing engaging pedagogy.

Swing (2002) also looked at seminar structure and found that colleges and universities are highly varied in the number of contact hours offered for these courses, from noncredit to more than three credits. Different levels of results were found for each of these categories. One-credit/contact-hour courses were as effective as courses with greater contact at introducing students to institutional policies and practices. However,

> [i]f the course goals also include increased knowledge of campus services, improvement in time management and other study skills, increasing student/ student and student/faculty connections, and increased out-of-class engagement, then at least 2 contact hours per week are more effective in producing these learning outcomes. If the course goals also include gains in academic skills and critical thinking, then a 3-contact hour course is more likely to produce the desired learning outcomes (Swing 2002, 1).

In summary, there are a range of options for the design and implementation of first-year seminars, and a preponderance of the research shows positive outcomes from student participation. However, while it has been said that "the first-year seminar is the most researched innovation in higher education" (Tobolowsky, Cox, and Wagner 2005, 5), there is still much that could be done to move the research in this area to the next level, which would benefit both students and institutions.

CHAPTER 2
Learning Communities

★ ★ ★ ★ ★ ★ ★ ★ ★ ★ ★ ★ ★ ★ ★ ★

WHILE THE EARLIEST LEARNING COMMUNITY INITIATIVE is commonly dated to the 1920s, learning communities (LCs) began to thrive in earnest during the past twenty years. Learning communities encompass a range of formats and definitions, but hundreds of colleges and universities now offer some form of this experience, and nearly 30 percent of first-year students who completed the National Survey of Student Engagement at doctoral-extensive and master's institutions reported participating in a learning community (Kuh et al. 2007). Residential LCs—often known as living-learning communities—in which LC students live together in a campus residence hall with additional resources, have also grown in popularity.

In their simplest form, learning communities are a collection of courses that a small group of students complete together. The courses are connected by a common theme, thereby encouraging students to see how knowledge is integrated across disciplines. Ideally, LCs are "integrated, comprehensive programs in which transformative learning takes place through a community process as students develop professional, civic, and ethical responsibility" (Brower and Dettinger 1998, 21). From the simplest LCs to those approaching ideal, the intended outcomes for LC students are the same.

These intended outcomes emerge in the LC literature. First, by placing a small group of students together in a common intellectual experience, an LC makes a large campus feel more intimate and provides students with an easily identifiable peer group. Second, by allowing students to get to know their classmates better, LCs engender the hope that students will feel more comfortable in the classroom and will take more intellectual risks and participate more fully in their classes. Third, LCs are typically designed to increase student interaction with faculty through small classes, often with out-of-class experiences. Fourth, LCs often use active and collaborative learning methods to increase student participation and ownership in the classroom. Fifth, linking courses for students aims to teach them how to look for connections among their classes so they will be able to integrate knowledge more effectively after leaving the LC. In summary, the goals of LCs are closely tied to the concepts of student involvement, student engagement, and the importance of integration into the social and academic environments of a college, each of which contributes to student learning and persistence (see, respectively, Astin 1984; Kuh, Schuh, and Whitt 1991; and Tinto 1993 for more information about these three concepts).

STUDENT OUTCOMES

LCs have been hailed as having many positive outcomes for both students and institutions, but it is relatively recently that researchers have begun testing the results of LC participation. Much of what has been written in this area is in the form of internal institutional reports evaluating a single campus's program. (For findings from a wide range of single-institution reports, see Taylor 2003.) The studies included in this chapter are primarily published articles, multi-institutional studies, or reports sponsored by foundations.

Outcomes for LCs can be broken into four main groups: (1) academic achievement and persistence, (2) behavioral outcomes, (3) attitudinal outcomes, and (4) outcomes associated with the goals of a liberal education.

Academic Achievement and Persistence

The outcomes that are the most direct and most commonly measured are retention or year-to-year persistence and grades or grade point averages, which are often referred to as a measure of academic achievement. Most studies in this group found that LC students had both higher grades and greater persistence than non-LC students. Others found higher grades and/or persistence, but the differences tended to be modest and often decreased over time.

Some findings in this area are quite encouraging. For example, in a multicampus, multiyear study of campuses that serve diverse, predominantly low-income and first-generation students, LC students had significantly higher rates of persistence than non-LC students—nearly 10 percent higher at four-year schools and more than 5 percent higher at two-year schools (Engstrom and Tinto 2008a). Even after controlling for demographics and engagement levels, differences in persistence were found (Engstrom and Tinto 2008b). Zheng et al. (2002) studied residential students, 40 percent of whom participated in an LC and 60 percent of whom did not. The authors found higher grades among LC participants as compared to their non-LC peers, even after controlling for demographics, precollege performance, and attitudinal and motivation factors. The authors concluded that self-selection did not contribute to the positive outcome.

When reviewing the background characteristics of students who chose to enroll or not enroll in a first-year LC at an urban, mainly commuter institution, Hotchkiss, Moore, and Pitts (2006) found that the LCs tended to enroll students who would typically perform more poorly academically than those in non-LC courses. That is, LC courses tended to attract academically weaker students. Given that difference, while the raw GPA and persistence data showed minimal differences between groups, after controlling for precollege background, LC participation had a greater-than-expected impact on the LC students. LC participation led to significantly higher retention than expected one year after matriculation for both black men and women. An investigation of GPA found that while white women in the LC performed about as would be predicted by the raw data, LC participation led to more than a full letter grade increase for black men (0.93 higher for black women, and 0.78 higher for white men). A year later, the GPA gap between LC and non-LC students narrowed, but was still significant (Hotchkiss, Moore, and Pitts 2006).

A few studies, including one by Barrows and Goodfellow (2005), examined persistence in science, math, or technology programs rather than in an institution as a whole. Their findings suggest that participation in an LC could be used as a tool to increase retention in these programs.

Taking a different approach, Lichtenstein (2005) looked at the effect of the quality of the classroom environment on grades and persistence for LC students, rather than looking at program participation alone. Students in classrooms that successfully linked content between classes, built a sense of community, and helped students build skills for future academic success had the highest grades and persistence over three terms. Students in negative classroom environments—defined as those in which professors in linked courses did not coordinate material and/or were in conflict, did not create community in or out of the classroom, and did not focus on skill development—had the lowest persistence and grades when comparing them to students in positive or mixed environments and to students not in an LC.

Behavioral Outcomes
Findings related to behavioral outcomes have also been mainly positive. LCs have been found to ease first-year students' transition to college. For example, Inkelas and Weisman (2003) studied three types of residential LCs on one college campus and found that regardless of participation in an honors community, a discipline-based community, or a residential LC specifically designed to ease the transition into college, all LC participants reported an easier transition to college than did non-LC students. LCs also have been helpful for community college students, who credited the positive peer environment of their LCs with the ease of their transition to college (Tinto 1997).

Multiple studies have found that both residential and nonresidential LCs ease the social and/or academic integration of students (Blackhurst, Akey, and Bobilya 2003; Inkelas et al. 2007; Pike, Schroeder, and Berry 1997). Tinto (1997) found that the LC community college students he studied described social integration as a necessary step that allowed them to focus on academic engagement. That finding led Tinto to speculate that persistence may be developmental in nature. That is, first-year students may need to focus on establishing social connections first, and once those are established, they may be more able to focus on their academic pursuits.

Faculty interaction and peer interaction are two of the most common behavioral outcomes examined in the LC literature, with most studies concluding that LC participation leads to increases in faculty–student interaction and peer-to-peer interaction both in and out of the classroom. For example, in studying thousands of LC and non-LC students who completed the NSSE survey in 2002, Zhao and Kuh (2004) found that LC students had more interaction with faculty and were more involved with active and collaborative learning.

Residential LC students are more likely to have faculty mentoring experiences than those in traditional residence halls (Inkelas, Johnson et al. 2006; Inkelas, Vogt et al. 2006), and are more likely to meet with faculty socially outside of class (Inkelas and Weisman 2003). LC students also have been found to experience more familiarity with and concern for their peers (Duran et al. 2005) and a greater sense of connection to their peers (Waldron and Yungbluth 2007). For LCs populated exclusively or predominantly by commuting students, the community structures inherent in the LCs provided an opportunity for students to have increased contact with both faculty and peers, compared to those students in traditional classrooms (Engstrom and Tinto 2008b; Waldron and Yungbluth 2007).

However, despite the increased faculty contact built into LCs, researchers also found that peer interaction sometimes trumped faculty interaction in significance for students. Studying multiple residential LCs on a single campus, some of which were designed to have greater faculty involvement, Schussler and Fierros (2008) found that no one residential LC group reported higher degrees of student–faculty interaction than any other. Yet, all residential LC students reported that the relationships they made with peers in their residence halls had a greater impact on their feeling of belonging than did relationships formed in the classroom.

In addition to these positive outcomes, a 2008 study by Jaffee et al. also found negative outcomes in LCs, namely, the formation of cliques and the perpetuation of a "high school feeling" through the first year of college. However, students who reported these negative outcomes also reported a higher sense of community and satisfaction than non-LC students.

Attitudinal Outcomes
While not universal, the majority of studies that looked at attitudinal outcomes were conducted with predominantly underserved populations or at community colleges. One theme that emerges among qualitative studies concerns the way the LC experience leads students to gain voice or grow in their identity as learners. In interviews and focus groups, students talked about LCs providing them with a safe space where they felt comfortable taking academic risks, participating in class, and finding their voices as learners (Engstrom and Tinto 2008a, 2008b).

Similar outcomes emerged from a multiculturally themed LC designed for TRIO students,[3] reported in two studies (James, Brush, and Jehangir 2006; Jehangir 2008). The TRIO students were predominantly first-generation, low-income students of color in their first term at a large university. By reviewing students' reflective journals and course papers, the authors found that the LC helped these students build identities as learners. The students discussed how the cluster allowed them to see that they had something to contribute in this environment and recognize their academic potential. Growth in academic self-confidence, a concept related to growing in one's identity as a learner, is also identified as a theme in the literature (Engstrom and Tinto 2008a; Inkelas, Vogt et al. 2006; Tinto and Love 1995).

LC participation contributes to a sense of belonging on a college campus. LC students discussed the importance of seeing students like themselves—commuting, first-generation, and low-income students—in their LCs. Developing relationships with their peers made them feel like they belonged at college and gave them confidence to participate and persist (Engstrom and Tinto 2008a).

Students' perceptions about support in the college environment was the one attitudinal outcome that was studied across a wide range of settings, and the findings were universally positive. Compared to students not in LCs, LC students felt a greater sense of encouragement (Engstrom and Tinto 2008a, 2008b) and felt that their campus was more supportive both academically and socially (Zhao and Kuh 2004). Tinto and Love (1995) found that, as compared to a matched non-LC cohort, LC students at a community college were more positive in their perceptions of their classes, faculty, the campus climate, and their own involvement. Residential LC students rated their residence halls as more academically and socially supportive than students in traditional housing rated their residence halls (Inkelas, Johnson et al. 2006; Inkelas, Vogt et al. 2006; Inkelas and Weisman 2003), and noted a more positive campus climate for racial and ethnic diversity (Inkelas, Vogt et al. 2006).

Liberal Education Outcomes

Critical thinking is an outcome commonly associated with liberal learning, and was the topic of several studies. However, while results were positive, nearly all these measures are based on student self-reported estimates of gains in critical thinking. Zhao and Kuh (2004) examined a range of outcomes that could be linked to critical thinking. When studying the national sample of NSSE first-year and senior respondents from 2002, they found that LC students reported greater gains in critical thinking and problem-solving skills, and took a greater number of courses that require higher-order thinking skills such as judging the quality of information and arguments, synthesis, and the application of theory.

Intellectual or cognitive development is different from critical thinking, and more likely to be measured using metrics other than self-reports. Within cognitive development theory, intellectual development is demonstrated by several measures, including an ability to see multiple points of view as valid, viewing both oneself and one's peers as valid sources of knowledge, seeing the potential for a teacher or professor to be a co-learner in the classroom, and understanding that knowledge is constructed (e.g., Baxter Magolda 1992; King and Kitchener 1994; Perry 1970). Avens and Zelley (1992) used Knefelkamp's (1974) and Widick's (1975) Measure of Intellectual Development (MID) to study a full-year, three-course LC at a community college. By analyzing student responses to the MID at the start, middle, and end of the term, Avens and Zelley found that students in the community college LC displayed more growth in intellectual development in one year than most students in national samples develop in four.

Using students' reflective journals and academic papers as the basis for analysis, two studies of a multiculturally themed LC designed for predominantly first-generation, low-income students in TRIO programs found similar outcomes (James, Bruch, and Jehangir 2006; Jehangir 2008). The

---

3. TRIO programs are federally funded programs that aim to assist and support students who are classified as low income, first-generation, and/or disabled. The programs assist both college-attending and college-bound students (Council for Opportunity in Education 2008).

authors noted that during the course of the semester, students came to see themselves and their peers as a source of knowledge, and to understand that diverse views led to a stronger learning environment—both of which are key indicators of intellectual development.

Researchers found that LC students felt more able to integrate information or make connections among classes than did non-LC students (Duran et al. 2005; Inkelas, Vogt et al. 2006). In fact, in interviews, students often mentioned that ability as one advantage of being in an LC (e.g., Dabney, Green, and Topali 2006; Engstrom and Tinto 2008a; Tinto and Love 1995).

Reading and writing skills, measured by self-report or by analysis of students' work, were another outcome studied. Duran et al. (2005) compared LC students with a matched sample that took the non-LC versions of the same courses. They asked students to assess their own skill development and then analyzed student writing from the courses. LC students self-reported greater gains in writing than did non-LC students. The writing analysis showed that LC students did, in fact, have greater improvement in writing quality and clarity, and the improvement demonstrated was even greater than in the self-report measure.

Another study used a different objective measure to examine this outcome. Researchers followed LC students at a community college, most of whom were taking developmental English as part of the LC (Scrivener et al. 2008). Compared to matched peers, the LC students were much more likely to pass developmental reading and writing tests after one term, allowing them to continue into credit-bearing college classes more quickly. Further, the non-LC group had not caught up in completion of the developmental sequence three terms later.

Engagement with diversity—defined as "the range of dimensions that individuals and groups bring to the educational experience" that can be applied to "the service of learning" (Clayton-Pedersen 2009)—is a significant area of inquiry in the literature. First, researchers looked at openness to new ideas in general or to diversity in particular, and found that LC participants tended to be more open to new ideas than their non-LC peers (Inkelas, Johnson et al. 2006; Inkelas, Vogt et al. 2006; Inkelas and Weisman 2003; Pike 2002).

However, not all changes found in this area were positive. In one quantitative study of a civic engagement–themed residential LC, Longerbeam and Sedlacek (2006) found some regression in attitudes regarding racial and ethnic diversity (2006). The authors note that regression can be a normal part of the developmental process, and that a more longitudinal, qualitative study might be necessary to track long-term changes for this outcome before drawing definite conclusions.

In other studies reviewing diversity outcomes, residential LC students nationwide were found to be more likely than those in traditional residence halls to participate in diversity-related activities (Inkelas, Johnson et al. 2006) and to engage in sociocultural conversations with peers (Inkelas, Vogt et al. 2006; Inkelas and Weisman 2003). From the national sample of first-year and senior respondents of the NSSE survey, LC students—residential and nonresidential—were found to engage in more diversity-related activities than non-LC students (Zhao and Kuh 2004).

Only one study measured civic engagement as an outcome. Rowan-Kenyon, Soldner, and Inkelas (2007) used a three-pronged definition of civic engagement encompassing civic knowledge, values, and skills. It includes service to others, a belief in personal responsibility, and a sense of responsibility for the common good. Using this definition, the authors examined civic engagement of students in a general residential LC, a civic engagement-themed residential LC, and a traditional residence hall, all of whom completed the National Survey of Living Learning Programs. After controlling for demographic variables and precollege attitudes about the importance of cocurricular involvement, students in the civic engagement residential LC had higher rates of civic engagement, followed by those in other residential LCs.

LCs have been shown to contribute to gains in personal and social development, including developing an understanding of oneself and of others different from oneself, and the development of values and ethics (Zhao and Kuh 2004).

OUTCOMES FOR UNDERSERVED STUDENTS

Some of the authors above have sought to determine the outcomes for specific groups of underserved populations. It could be argued that every community college study falls under this category, since it is in two-year institutions that many students of color, first-generation students, and low-income students begin or complete their college careers. Those studies tell us that LCs play an important role both for students from historically underserved groups in community colleges, and for the community college context as a whole. They play a part in creating a sense of support and community for students who may not feel that they belong in a college environment, either because of their level of high school preparation or because they have many conflicts that arise from their home, work, and/or school demands. This support leads students to take more academic risks by actively participating in classes and finding opportunities for growth and learning, and by listening to diverse views and voices in the classroom. Avens and Zelley (1992) and Tinto (1997) found that through these experiences, students' views of knowledge were broadened and they made notable gains in intellectual development. These LC community college students were more likely to report that their faculty cared about and believed in their success, and they had greater levels of peer and faculty interaction than matched non-LC peers, when studied (Engstrom and Tinto 2008a, 2008b). Similar results were found in an LC at a four-year school designed for TRIO students, which included mainly low-income, first-generation students, over 90 percent of whom were also students of color (James, Bruch, and Jehangir 2006; Jehangir 2008).

Another set of studies looked specifically at a single category of underserved students, or broke down their analysis by demographic group. For example, Inkelas et al. (2007) found that first-generation students in residential LCs experienced an easier academic and social transition than first-generation students in traditional residence halls. However, they also found that time spent on integration into the academic realm of college had a somewhat negative effect on social integration, possibly because time spent on academics reduced the time available for cocurricular involvement. Since integration into both the social and academic realms of campus has been found to be a necessary condition for student persistence, academic integration at the cost of social integration is a concern (Tinto 1993). Interestingly, while these students' actual interactions with peers seemed to have little impact on their transition to college, perceptions of a positive peer environment were very significant for these students. The authors found no significant differences among this group's outcomes based on gender, race/ethnicity, generational status in the United States, or income.

Inkelas and Weisman (2003), in their study of three types of residential LCs and a non-residential LC control group, found that African American and Latino students in a residential LC for honor students experienced a smoother transition to college than non-residential LC students from those ethnic/racial groups. Women and African American students in the non-residential LC group reported less openness to different social or cultural perspectives than these student populations in a transition, honors, or discipline-based residential LC. Latino students in the discipline-based residential LC were the most open to those new perspectives as compared to Latino students in any other population studied.

MODERATING VARIABLES

One of the challenges in reviewing specific outcomes of LCs is that these studies cover all types of LCs and various target populations. It would be helpful to know whether particular types of LCs lead to different outcomes.

Among nonresidential communities, all LCs consist of linked or clustered courses, but a few other distinctions are possible, such as the number of courses linked, and the presence or absence of a first-year or integrative seminar. However, much of the research does not specify the exact nature of the LC program studied, making it difficult to say with certainty how these differences affect outcomes. In addition, authors often group several LC formats together in one study.

Residential LC programs are particularly problematic for analysis. Few of the studies specify the details of the curricular component of the residential LC program, and since most of the residential LC studies use multi-institutional data, those differences are impossible to determine. Unlike nonresidential LCs, residential LCs do not always link multiple courses to each other, but sometimes link just one course to a residential experience on the same theme. Further, some residential LCs do not have a curricular component at all, but are actually themed housing. When possible, such residential LCs were excluded from this review.

Despite these challenges in the literature, the research shows that regardless of the type of LC, positive outcomes appear to result. Whether highly structured programs with a range of support services attached or just two courses connected by a common theme, residentially based or not, students benefit from LC participation.

Importantly, the range and intensity (i.e., the variability) of outcomes are influenced by the quality of the LC, more than by LC type. All LCs appear to lead to increased faculty and peer interaction, and LC students will be able to integrate their learning more effectively than when taking discrete courses, simply because material across courses is labeled with a common theme and therefore connected. Just as any on-campus residential experience has been shown to have a positive effect on students (e.g., Pascarella, Terenzini, and Bliming 1994), residential LCs have some benefits beyond LCs alone, merely by the nature of students spending more time together and continuing their classroom conversations in the residence halls. However, as Lichtenstein (2005) demonstrated, a negative learning environment in an LC will lead to the same outcome (or worse) than no LC at all, while intentional, positive environments will benefit students and institutions in many ways. Especially for students who are the first in their families to attend college, who commute and spend limited time on campus, who are low income and often need to work significant hours while going to school, and/or who are academically underprepared for college at entry, intentionally arranged LCs that integrate learning while also connecting students to each other and to their institution's resources can make a significant difference in students' persistence, views of themselves, and their learning.

CHAPTER 3

Service Learning

★ ★ ★ ★ ★ ★ ★ ★ ★ ★ ★ ★ ★ ★ ★ ★

IN THEORY AND IN PRACTICE, service learning has many permutations, and each institution may define service learning differently, depending on its formulation of the practice. Crews (2002, viii) remarks: "Given its flexibility and the many different ways in which it is being experimented with in vastly different contexts and communities, service learning certainly can be seen as a set of pedagogies" as opposed to a singular practice. Despite this variability within the field, Jacoby (1996, 5) offers the following definition: "Service-learning is a form of experiential education in which students engage in activities that address human and community needs together with structured opportunities intentionally designed to promote student learning and development." Stanton, Giles, and Cruz (1999, 2) hold that the essence of service learning lies in its name, which "joins two complex concepts: community action, the 'service,' and efforts to learn from that action and connect what is learned to existing knowledge, the 'learning.'"

"SERVICE" IN SERVICE LEARNING

In most service-learning practices, students are generally involved in service through unpaid work in a community setting. Community can be defined in various ways and might be local, national, or international; service to the campus community itself, however, is generally not accepted as viable for a service-learning experience. Common examples of service-learning settings include homeless shelters, immigrant centers, health clinics, legal aid agencies, and other community organizations. While students perform a wide range of duties in these settings, ranging from clerical work to direct contact with the constituencies served, Eyler and Giles (1999) assert that the more relevant the service is to the student's coursework, the more meaningful the learning experience can become.

Regardless of its particular formulation, all service-learning programs reflect a philosophical stance toward those being served (Hoppe 2004). A *philanthropic* perspective views the educational goal of service learning as instilling in students a spirit of charity, which in turn will inspire students to continue to give to those less fortunate over their lifetimes. This perspective operates from a deficit model, in which the community being served is deficient in some area, which deficiency is then provided for by student service. The *civic* perspective, however, views service as founded on democratic principles, with students serving as agents of change to help empower community members. A social-justice orientation, which challenges existing power structures that lead to disenfranchisement and oppression of the community being served, is generally consonant with the civic perspective. The *communitarian* perspective holds that through service, students can become responsible members of communities and work toward shared values that lead to self-governance (Codispoti 2004).

The philosophical basis in which a particular service-learning experience is grounded is an important consideration in designing and implementing service-learning programs. Not only can it affect the structure of the experience, it can also shape students' learning and experiences related to service. This is true for students from all backgrounds, and yet special attention should be paid to the experience of underrepresented students, who may have similar backgrounds as those receiving service (Myers-Lipton 2002). For example, service learning operating from a deficit model may alienate and further disempower students from historically underrepresented groups, whereas service learning operating from a civic or communitarian perspective may empower students for learning, identity development, and community action.

"LEARNING" IN SERVICE LEARNING

Throughout the literature, service learning is described as a pedagogy that utilizes active learning and integrates students' curricular learning with their experiences of service. This type of integrative service learning has been implemented in a wide range of academic disciplines and professional fields (Madden 2000); a monograph series by the American Association for Higher Education covers formulations of service learning in fields and disciplines such as biology, composition, engineering, history, management, philosophy, political science, psychology, and others. Zlotkowski (1999) highlights the importance of the faculty's role, regardless of academic discipline, in articulating the rationale, purpose, and learning goals of service activities, as well as ensuring that the specific tasks of service are relevant to those goals.

In terms of course activities, much of the service-learning literature points to structured opportunities for reflection, such as journal writing and group discussion, as the hallmarks of the pedagogy. Eyler and Giles (1999, 171) explain that, "At its simplest, reflection is being able to step back and be thoughtful about experience—to monitor one's own reactions and thinking processes." On a more complex level, reflection enables students not only to make connections between their classroom learning and their service experiences, but also to consider the meaning of their learning and how it may be applied to both enduring and contemporary social challenges.

OUTCOMES OF SERVICE LEARNING

The literature on student outcomes related to involvement in service learning points to multidimensional change in students as a result of participation. Roldan, Strage, and David (2004) provide a helpful categorization of these types of outcomes into three broad categories: academic achievement, civic engagement, and personal growth.

Academic Achievement

There is reasonably strong evidence in the literature that service learning has a positive effect on many aspects of students' learning. Astin, Sax, and Avalos (1999) surveyed forty-two institutions involved in the Learn and Serve America Program and found that participation in service was associated with higher grade point averages, greater retention, a greater likelihood of degree completion, and more interaction with faculty, alongside gains in academic knowledge. Berson and Younkin (1998) found that community college students engaged in service learning obtained significantly higher course grades and also reported higher levels of satisfaction with their learning experience.

In *Where's the Learning in Service-Learning?* Eyler and Giles (1999) report similar findings from two comprehensive studies of service-learning outcomes, one involving extensive surveys of 1,500 students and the other involving intensive student interviews of a smaller sample. Specifically, in the area of understanding and applying knowledge, students reported that they were motivated to work harder in service-learning classes, experienced deeper understanding of subject matter and social issues, and were better able to apply classroom learning to real problems. With regard to critical-thinking skills, Eyler and Giles report that students "in service-learning classes where service and learning are well integrated through classroom focus and reflection are more likely to show an increase in their level of critical thinking demonstrated in problem analysis" (127).

Civic Engagement

A range of studies indicate that participation in service learning can yield substantial gains in civic engagement, which include cognitive, attitudinal, and behavioral aspects. Examples of these aspects are recognizing the needs in one's community (cognitive), believing one has the capacity to effect change in the community (attitudinal), and participating in a community clean-up effort (behavioral). Eyler and Giles (1999) found that a third of service-learning participants reported gaining a new perspective on social issues, and that service learning had an effect on students' perceptions of the locus of social problems, valuing of social justice, and desire personally to effect political change. Eyler and Giles claim that these and other identified outcomes of service learning contribute to "active and effective citizenship," which they describe as comprised of the elements of values, knowledge, skills, efficacy, and commitment (163). Similarly, Myers-Lipton (1998) found that those engaged in course-based service learning (as opposed to non-course-linked community service or no service) experienced significant gains in their locus of control, civic behavior, and concern for civic responsibility, while these outcomes for students in the non-course-linked service group or those participating in no service stayed the same or even declined.

Personal Growth

Eyler and Giles (1999) found that participation in service learning led to reduced stereotyping and greater tolerance, as well as student reports of positive effect on their ability to work well with others. Participation in service learning was a predictor of increased leadership skills and, in affective terms, students reported "greater self-knowledge, spiritual growth, and finding reward in helping others" as a result of service-learning participation (55). The authors also point to service learning as a "predictor of an increased sense of personal efficacy" and "desire to include service to others in one's career plans" (55). Additionally, participation in service learning was a predictor of students' feeling connected to the community and a means of creating opportunity for close relationships among students and between faculty and students.

In a study of more than twenty thousand students utilizing Cooperative Institutional Research Program (CIRP) data, Astin et al. (2000, iv) explain that "service learning is effective in part because it facilitates four types of outcomes: an increased sense of personal efficacy, an increased awareness of the world, an increased awareness of one's personal values, and increased engagement in the classroom experience."

Finally, there is some evidence that participation in service learning is correlated with better health-related behaviors. Wechsler et al. (1995), Jessor et al. (1995), and Fenzel (2005) all describe a correlation between participation in prosocial activities like community service and lower rates of alcohol consumption. However, since it is unclear whether students who were predisposed to drink less alcohol had self-selected into service-learning experiences, Fenzel asserts, "cause and effect cannot be inferred" (136).

OUTCOMES FOR UNDERSERVED STUDENTS

Very little research has been conducted on the effect of service learning on students from underserved groups. As Myers-Lipton (2002) explains, "The limitation of service-learning, both in research and in practice, is that the focus has been primarily on European American students" and often these students are from middle-class or affluent socioeconomic backgrounds (202). Despite this reality, the few studies that have been conducted point to the benefits of service learning for students from underrepresented groups.

Outcomes for Students of Color

One of the most frequently cited studies is that of Roose et al. (1997), who conducted a retention study of African American students who attended Oberlin College from 1987 to 1991. Involvement in community service was the factor most strongly correlated with graduation, out of a total of fifteen variables studied.

Beyond the issue of retention, some studies have demonstrated academic gains for students of color engaged in service learning. For example, in a study of sociology students at a historically black institution, Balazadeh (1996) found that students who chose to enroll in a sociology course involving service learning had better grade performance compared with those who did not (thus self-selection bias was an issue). Tartter (1996) also found that the GPAs of undergraduate students who mentored second-graders in an urban public school increased, on average, by 0.14 points.

Studies that examined the civic engagement of students of color in service learning are also limited and sometimes contradictory in their findings. Mabry (1998), in a study of students participating in service learning in twenty-three different courses, found that men, nonwhite participants and those students with the least service experience showed significant positive changes in their civic attitudes as a result of participation in service learning. Smedick (1996), however, surveyed alumni and found that African Americans and women who had participated in service during college were more service-oriented than European Americans or Asian Americans who had participated as well. Boyle-Baise and Langford (2004), in a study of an alternative spring break service-learning class, found that activist views were more common for students of color than for white students. Taken cumulatively, these findings suggest that more research is needed on civic outcomes for students of color who participate in service learning.

Although indirectly related to outcomes, there have been some studies of the perceptions and experiences of students of color engaged in service learning. Pickron-Davis (1999) found that black students who worked with lower-class, black middle school students in a service-learning context reported the absence of critical dialogue on race and cultural differences in their classes, that they self-silenced when issues of race were raised in class, and that they experienced dual identities as college students and as role models and service providers in the middle schools. Similarly, Einfeld and Collins (2008), in a qualitative study of an AmeriCorps program, found that students may have differential outcomes in terms of their orientation toward social justice or toward charity in the service setting; the authors found that while all participants "acknowledged and witnessed inequality…some participants developed a social justice paradigm [civic perspective] and others adopted a charity paradigm [philanthropic perspective]. It is possible that these differences in paradigms were the result of varied backgrounds…" (104).

There is also evidence that the experiences of students of color in service learning are significantly different from those of white students. For example, Myers-Lipton (2002) conducted a study of a sociology course in which seventeen out of twenty-eight students were students of color. Fifteen of those twenty-eight students participated in the study and completed integration papers and a questionnaire. From analyzing these data sources, Myers-Lipton concluded that "students of color experience service learning in ways that are different from and similar to (but with different results) European American students," particularly in their insights and responses to those being served (216). Students related differently to clients because "they see part of themselves in the people with whom they are working. This insight about 'sameness' may also lead students of color to explore their own ethnic identity as well as develop a strong commitment to racial and social justice" (216). Myers-Lipton concludes that attention should be paid to the potential differences in experiences among service-learning participants.

Low-Income and First-Generation College Students

The only research found pertinent to first-generation students and those from low-income backgrounds addressed the issue that such students do not often participate in service learning. Horn et al. (1995), in their study of 66,000 students for the 1992-1993 National Postsecondary Student Aid Study, report that high income and high parental education levels were correlated with likelihood of students performing service. In a two-year study of eleven sociology courses, in which students were offered the opportunity to perform service or choose another project, Ender et al. (2000) found that off-campus students who worked were less likely than any other group to choose the service option. And Zawacki (1997) found that, in a group of students divided into three subgroups (service learning related to a course, no service, and prior service not related to a course), students whose mothers had at least a college degree were more likely to volunteer. Together, these studies show that since service learning is usually optional, it is often selected by those students who have the time to involve themselves in service, which often means residential students who do not work, or who work part time on campus. Those students who commute, work off campus, and/or have family responsibilities may have less time and inclination to participate in a course-based service experience that is not required for academic credit.

MODERATING VARIABLES

The performance of community service by college students takes many forms throughout higher education. Thus, we must consider what variables in the formulation of service experiences affect outcomes. First and foremost in this discussion is whether service learning itself, as opposed to cocurricular volunteerism, has added benefit for students. In their meta-analysis of higher education research, Pascarella and Terenzini (2005), when considering the different formulations of service-oriented activities, found support for the hypothesis that "greater learning will occur in courses or curricula where the service component is an integral part of the course content and activities and where there is a regular reflective component linking the two (that is, service learning) than in courses that simply contain a service component…" (129–30).

Vogelgesang and Astin (2000), in their study of over twenty thousand students using CIRP data, found that students in course-based service demonstrated significant gains over those in generic community service in the development of cognitive skills, choosing a service-related career, commitment to activism, and promoting racial understanding. Utilizing CIRP data again, Astin et al. (2000, ii) found that performing service as part of a course "*adds* significantly to the benefits associated with community service" (italics in original), namely in the development of academic skills, choice of a service career, and plans to participate in service after college.

Given the diversity of service-learning practices across institutions of higher education, the quality of these practices is particularly important. As Eyler and Giles (1999, xvii) explain, "Service-learning makes a difference, and within the group who experience these programs, higher-quality service-learning makes a bigger difference." Roldan, Strage, and David (2004), in their review of related service-learning research, concluded that a higher number of service hours, direct contact with clients, careful planning and preparation, successful partnerships with community sites, orientation and supervision of students, and reflection activities all seem to enhance student outcomes in service learning. From their analysis of CIRP data, Astin et al. (2000) report that moderating variables include student interest in the subject (thus supporting the use of service learning in the major), professors' encouragement of class discussion, the connection between the service experience and the course content, and the use of reflection. Mabry (1998) similarly concluded that service learning is more effective when it involves at least fifteen to twenty hours of service, frequent contact with the community members receiving service, weekly reflection in class, formative and summative written reflection, and student discussion of experiences with instructors and site supervisors. Finally, Batchelder and Root (1994) found that onsite supervision and quality of instruction were important mediating variables for the outcomes they identified (moral cognition and reasoning, and development of occupational identity).

CHAPTER 4

Undergraduate Research

★ ★ ★ ★ ★ ★ ★ ★ ★ ★ ★ ★ ★ ★ ★ ★

UNDERGRADUATE RESEARCH CAN BE CHARACTERIZED as "a growing movement [that] transcends institutional boundaries and types" (Kinkead 2005, 7). This movement largely has its origin in the "scientific community [which], appalled by the number of reports proclaiming the scientific illiteracy of American students, embarked on a national campaign to ground instruction in science and mathematics" in the 1980s and 1990s (7). Reports and a strategic plan provided by the National Science Foundation, along with the report of the Boyer Commission on Educating Undergraduates in the Research University, *Reinventing Undergraduate Education: A Blueprint for America's Research Universities* (1998), provided the catalyst for the establishment of undergraduate research programs at institutions throughout the country (for a detailed history of the undergraduate research movement, see Merkel 2001.) Although undergraduate research had its inception in the sciences, such opportunities now frequently extend to the arts, humanities, and social sciences. (For examples of undergraduate research across multiple disciplines, see Karukstis and Elgren 2007, Kaufman and Stocks 2004, and Lee 2004.)

Out of the several high-impact practices discussed in this review, undergraduate research has most often been targeted to underrepresented students in higher education. Many institutions have utilized forms of undergraduate research, such as undergraduate research opportunity programs or summer research opportunity programs, to engage students of color, as well as academically underserved students, in the scholarly enterprise.

Defining Undergraduate Research

Kinkead (2005, 6) asserts that "*undergraduate research* is defined broadly to include scientific inquiry, creative activity, and scholarship," and many hold that the student's work should be original and make a contribution to the student's discipline (Hu et al. 2008). Undergraduate research opportunities are generally structured in nature and are often sponsored or administrated by the student's major department. Some institutions have undergraduate research centers or may house related programs within broader teaching and learning centers. A number of national organizations—the Council on Undergraduate Research; the National Conferences on Undergraduate Research; Project Kaleidoscope; and the Center for the Integration of Research, Teaching, and Learning—also support students, faculty, and institutions engaged in undergraduate research.

As a pedagogy, undergraduate research is fundamentally different from traditional forms of teaching in the academy. This is underscored by the report of the Boyer Commission (1998, 15), which asserts that "learning is based on discovery guided by mentoring rather than on the transmission of information." In such a model, undergraduates would be responsible for co-creating knowledge through the process of inquiry, as opposed to receiving, memorizing, and re-presenting knowledge from faculty experts. The commission asserts that "every course in an undergraduate curriculum should provide an opportunity for a student to succeed through discovery-based methods" (17).

Honor students, students of color, and academically disadvantaged students are populations to which undergraduate research opportunities are most systematically extended (Kinkead 2005). These opportunities are often called undergraduate research opportunity programs, and frequently employ a combination of faculty, graduate student, and upper-class student mentors. Other program features may include cognitive and skill development, writing, and presentation skills. Examples of such programs include those at the University of Michigan and the University of California, Los Angeles. In addition, the federally funded Ronald E. McNair Postbaccalaureate Achievement Program, a TRIO program that prepares students for eventual doctoral work, sponsors undergraduate research opportunities for students from disadvantaged backgrounds across many institutions.

Outcomes of Undergraduate Research

Compared to some of the other high-impact practices examined in this review, the literature on undergraduate research is not as extensive, especially in the area of student outcomes, and particularly beyond questions of retention and graduate school enrollment. In their meta-analysis of higher education research, Pascarella and Terenzini (2005, 406–7) found that undergraduate research has a "positive influence" on "persistence and degree completion," as well as "elevates degree aspirations…and the likelihood of enrolling in graduate school." However, other outcomes, such as those related to student learning, were not as well established.

Hu et al. (2008) summarize the known outcomes of undergraduate research, which include improvement in writing and communication skills, increased frequency and quality of interaction with faculty and peers, gains in problem solving and critical thinking, higher levels of satisfaction with the educational experience, and greater chance of enrollment in graduate school. Key studies to this effect include that of Bauer and Bennett (2003), who surveyed nearly one thousand graduates—418 who had participated in institutional research programs, 213 who worked on their own with faculty members, and 355 who had no research experience—and found that those in the first two groups (who were engaged in undergraduate research) were more likely to enroll in graduate school and reported a higher level of satisfaction with their undergraduate experience. They also reported gains in intellectual curiosity as well as research, communication, and time-management skills. Similarly, Russell, Hancock, and McCullough (2007) describe the results of a nationwide assessment of students who were funded by the National Science Foundation, and found that research experience increased students' interest in a science, technology, or engineering career, as well as in obtaining a PhD.

In a qualitative study, Seymour et al. (2004) found that among students at four liberal arts colleges, those involved in undergraduate research self-reported gains in (by frequency of occurrence): the personal and professional realm (including increased confidence as a researcher and collegial relationships with mentors and peers); "thinking and working like a scientist," (including critical thinking and problem solving); skill development (including skills in communication, writing, lab/field techniques, work organization, computer usage, reading comprehension, working collaboratively, and information retrieval); clarification and confirmation of career and graduate school plans; enhanced preparation for career or graduate school; and shifts in attitudes toward learning and working as a researcher (including learning to work independently, taking responsibility for learning, and a greater interest in/motivation for learning).

Lopatto (2006), in a study of summer research programs at four liberal arts colleges, described students' self-reported gains on a variety of skills related to research, ranging from research and hypothesis design to data collection and interpretation. In addition to research skills, students reported professional development—such as publication and presentation opportunities, resume building, and mentorship opportunities—as well as "understanding professional behavior, appreciating the demands of a career, and understanding how professionals work on problems" (23). Lopatto explains that these types of gains are often not noticed by faculty or tracked through programmatic assessment:

> Faculty mentors, especially those in science, often keep their focus on the payoff of
> undergraduate research for graduate school careers. But our research found
> evidence for a kind of development seen only out of the corner of the eye, so to
> speak. *Personal development*, including the growth of self-confidence, independence,
> tolerance for obstacles, interest in the discipline, and sense of accomplishment,

centers on the increasing understanding of one's self and one's capabilities. Undergraduate researchers reported gains on these dimensions and, when asked to indicate which benefits of undergraduate research were most important, included personal gains among those benefits (23, emphasis added).

These gains were reported regardless of the student's major, whether in the sciences, social sciences, arts, or humanities. In terms of mediating variables, Lopatto cites two conditions of faculty behavior as being important to the quality of students' experiences: "Two traits, 'responsive to your questions' and 'treats you like a colleague,' were directly correlated with the students' satisfaction with the research experience" (2006, 24).

OUTCOMES FOR UNDERSERVED STUDENTS

Issues of retention and graduate degree attainment are the focus of the majority of research conducted on the effects of undergraduate research participation for underserved populations (Nagda et al. 1998; Foertsch, Alexander, and Penberthy 2000; Ishiyama 2001). Pascarella and Terenzini (2005), in their meta-analysis of higher education research, report that undergraduate research has a positive effect on minority students' persistence, with the strongest effects on African American and sophomore students. Additionally, "Among minority students who pursued postbaccalaureate study, [undergraduate research] program participants were more likely to enter schools of medicine and law than were similar students who participated in less structured forms of undergraduate research" (407). Hu et al. (2008) also indicate that the majority of studies of undergraduate research and students from historically underrepresented groups, including first-generation students, address issues of retention and graduate school enrollment, and that the effects in these areas are positive.

There has been some research on the effect of undergraduate research for students from underrepresented groups beyond the concerns of retention and graduate school attendance. Jonides et al. (1992) conducted a study of the first year of the undergraduate research opportunities program (UROP) at the University of Michigan, which involved underrepresented minority students in the program, a primary control group of African American UROP applicants, and a secondary control group of white residential students. The authors found that:

> Students in UROP show higher levels of personal and collective self-esteem, they report more confidence in their research abilities and a greater likelihood of seeking an advanced degree, and they state that they are more likely to seek help from faculty and teaching assistants than students in either control group (11).

The influence of self-esteem was deemed to be "indirect… primarily through its influence on the coping strategies and confidence it provides" (12). In a subsequent study of the same program, Jonides (1995) found not only higher retention rates for program students than for underrepresented students university-wide, but also higher grade point averages (on average 6 percent) and positive effects on self-esteem, coping strategies, learning behaviors, and expectations about academic performance.

MODERATING VARIABLES

There has been little examination of the variables that may affect the actual learning experiences of students involved in undergraduate research. The relationship between the mentoring faculty member and the student is a logical consideration as a moderating variable, as this relationship is absolutely central to the undergraduate research experience. It can be "particularly meaningful to students deemed 'at risk,' including first-generation college students and minorities" (Elgren and Hensel 2006, 4).

Along these lines, Ishiyama (2007) utilized Lopatto's (2004) methodology to examine students in a program run by the Ronald E. McNair Postbaccalaureate Achievement Program. These students were from three groups: first-generation white/Caucasian students from low-income backgrounds; first-generation African American students from low-income backgrounds; and "continuing generation" African American students (i.e., those who had a parent or parents who completed college). The study specifically looked at students' characterizations of the mentoring relationship with faculty. Findings indicated that at least initially, African American students from both groups were more likely than white students to highlight the personal consideration role of mentors (listening to students' personal concerns, being a good listener, and being a friend) and the psychological benefits of undergraduate research; and to describe a good mentor as being personally supportive and concerned with the student's welfare. Ishiyama found that, over time, the first two emphases diminished, but the third persisted. Thus, the quality of the mentoring relationship may have an impact on the effectiveness of the undergraduate research experience.

CHAPTER 5

Capstone Courses and Projects

★ ★ ★ ★ ★ ★ ★ ★ ★ ★ ★ ★ ★ ★ ★ ★

ACCORDING TO GARDNER AND VAN DER VEER (1998, 15), capstone experiences are "summative curricular approaches such as courses synthesizing all of the content to date within a particular major (and often attempting to connect that concept back to the institution's basic theme of general education and the liberal arts)." Such opportunities—including classes, theses, final projects, internships, or artistic shows or recitals—were popularized in higher education literature and practice during the 1990s. For example, capstone experiences were highlighted in the report of the Boyer Commission on Educating Undergraduates in the Research University (1998, 27), which urged that students' "final semester(s) should focus on a major project and utilize to the fullest the research and communication skills learned in the previous semesters."

In addition to the Boyer Commission's report, the late 1990s also saw a focus on "the senior-year experience" as initiated by the National Resource Center for the First-Year Experience and Students in Transition at the University of South Carolina. Gardner, Van der Veer, and Associates' publication, *The Senior Year Experience* (1998), brought attention to the use of capstone experiences as a way to provide opportunities for integration, application, and closure to the senior year—and in some cases, to a student's entire academic career. During the past decade, however, discussion of capstone experiences appears to have declined; one possible explanation is that many of these experiences have been subsumed into the larger and now more visible category of "undergraduate research" (Lopatto 2006).

Defining Capstone Courses and Projects

Heinemann (1997, 2) identifies a major difficulty in defining capstone experiences in higher education: "There are undoubtedly more variations of content for the senior capstone course than for any other common course taught by colleges and universities." This is seen even in the contradictory definitions offered in the literature. Some authors describe the focus of capstones as integrating learning already obtained, while others frame capstones as opportunities to apply and expand learning to real-world situations of practice—although both purposes are not mutually exclusive. Furthermore, there is the question of *what learning* is at the focus of the capstone—learning in the major, learning in general education, or an integration of both. Henscheid (2000, 4) seems to suggest that higher education aims to attain a number of goals through the capstone experience, such as "to cement the student's disciplinary affiliation, to provide a rite of passage into the world of work or graduate school as a member of a distinct scholarly community, and to integrate the skills and knowledge acquired in the discipline."

Regardless of their purpose or focus, capstone experiences may take multiple formulations. Levine (1998) classifies these formulations into three types: senior seminars, which vary widely by topic and quality; comprehensive examinations, which are less common; and senior theses or projects, which involve independent study and prepare students for the world of work or graduate school. In addition, at some institutions, students develop comprehensive portfolios that reflect their work from their total college experience, in their major, and/or in internship experiences. Henscheid (2000) conducted a large-scale study of 707 institutions and their use of capstone experiences. This study found that 70.3 percent of the capstone experiences were discipline or department based, 16.3 percent were interdisciplinary, 5.8 percent were transition courses (preparing for work, graduate school, or life after college), 4.6 percent were classified as "other," and 3 percent were career-planning courses.

According to Henscheid's findings, of six goals listed by study participants, the most common goal of senior seminars and capstone courses was to foster integration and synthesis within the academic major, which was cited four times more than connecting the academic major to the work world (the second most frequently cited goal). Other common goals were improving seniors' career preparation and preprofessional development, and promoting integration and connections between general education and the academic major. In summary, Henscheid (2000, 4) notes that capstone courses "are generally designed to leave students with an understanding of and appreciation for single academic disciplines." Henscheid also found that capstone experiences are generally not experiential in nature, so students who are engaged in capstones often do not have the opportunity to "practice the ideas and skills they have learned out in the workplace or community" (140–141).

Outcomes of Capstone Courses and Projects

Very few studies regarding the outcomes of participation in capstone courses were identified, whether for general or historically underserved student populations. Those studies identified typically involved a single major or capstone course (e.g., Stephen, Parente, and Brown 2002; Andreasen and Trede 1998). Most involved student self-reports of satisfaction with and gains from the experience, and while generally positive, it is hard to gauge the impact of capstone experiences through these small-scale studies. The notable exception is the National Survey of Student Engagement (NSSE), which annually gauges student participation in capstone experiences; the 2009 survey found that one-third of senior respondents engaged in a senior capstone, and the majority of those students reported primarily cognitive gains from their participation (NSSE 2009). The 2007 administration findings provide some insight into moderating variables; students' self-report data indicated that the following factors increased student gains in multiple desired outcomes: greater investment of time; the requirement of a final product or performance; relationship with the faculty member (e.g., frequent meetings, clear expectations, and helpful feedback); and collaboration with peers (National Survey of Student Engagement 2007). Experiential opportunities were also significant; of the various types of capstone experiences, field placements were correlated with gains in the greatest number of NSSE desired outcome areas.

Concluding Thoughts

While it is difficult to pinpoint a single reason for the lack of outcomes research on capstone experiences, certainly the aforementioned lack of an accepted definition or set of criteria for capstones in higher education is a major concern. To advance the field's understanding of the potential impact of these experiences, practitioners and researchers would be best served by developing such a definition or set of criteria on which to base programmatic development and assessment. One potential exemplar worth examining is that put forth by the University of California–Berkeley, which provides perhaps the most integrative view by envisioning capstones as the culmination of a three-stage process (exposure, experience, and capstone) in the undergraduate career (The Regents of the University of California at Berkeley 2003). According to the Regents, in the final stage of this process, the capstone, students "marshal the skills needed to develop their own research or creative questions and to initiate investigations and explorations the outcome of which is largely unknown." While the level of independence (collaboration with a team versus working alone) varies by discipline, students in the capstone "organize and synthesize knowledge and skills acquired in a wide array of settings and situations in the course of their undergraduate career under the guidance of a mentor." The capstone itself provides the opportunity for students to present their work, though the audience may vary (e.g., scholarly publication, professional conference, student conference/journal).

CHAPTER 6
Integrated Approaches

★ ★ ★ ★ ★ ★ ★ ★ ★ ★ ★ ★ ★ ★ ★ ★

EACH OF THE EDUCATIONAL ACTIVITIES REVIEWED in the previous chapters contributes to a range of positive outcomes for students, faculty, and institutions. There is also evidence that a combination of these activities may lead to even stronger outcomes.

LEARNING COMMUNITIES AND FIRST-YEAR SEMINARS

Of the 968 institutions that participated in the 2006 survey conducted by the National Resource Center on the First-Year Experience and Students in Transition, 85 percent reported offering a first-year seminar on their campus. Thirty-five percent of those link the seminars to one or more other courses as part of a learning community (LC). Looking at the studies that compare LCs with and without a linked first-year seminar, it is clear that adding a seminar not only adds different course material, but also typically adds a range of support services for students. Instructional teams made up of some combination of faculty, academic advisers, student affairs professionals, librarians, and information technology staff are common.

The research comparing stand-alone first-year seminars and those linked to an LC support the contention that these connections lead to better outcomes for students. For example, students from fourteen campuses that offer both stand-alone and linked seminars completed the 2002 First-Year Initiative Benchmarking Survey conducted by the Policy Center on the First Year of College, allowing for comparison between models (Swing 2004). Students in linked seminars were found to have significantly greater gains than those in stand-alone seminars on all ten of the learning outcomes studied. The most significant gains were in peer-to-peer connections, out-of-class engagement, knowledge of wellness issues, study skills, and time/priority management. Significant results were also found for knowledge of campus policies and academic services, critical thinking and cognitive/academic skills, and connections with faculty. Further, these students reported more experience with engaging pedagogies in the classroom, and were more satisfied with college than were their peers in stand-alone seminars.

Single-institution studies also found positive results. Among those is Tinto and Goodsell's (1993) examination of students who were enrolled in two learning communities at a large four-year university. The LCs consisted of two large lecture classes and a writing course. The LCs varied in that one included a writing seminar that integrated information from the other linked courses, and the other included a composition class that did not integrate that information. The LC students were compared to students who were enrolled in non-LC versions of the same classes. The authors found that while both LC groups had more positive outcomes than non-LC students, those with the integrative writing seminar were more actively involved in their classes, had more interaction with their faculty, were more involved on campus, and were more positive about their college experiences than were either of the other two groups.

Henscheid's monograph *Integrating the First-Year Experience: The Role of First-Year Seminars in Learning Communities* (2004) profiles fourteen two-year and four-year institutions that have intentionally connected first-year seminars and LCs. While the type of seminars vary school to school and the quality of the program assessment varies, these institutions report positive results for participants, including increased retention and grade point averages, feelings of a positive campus climate and satisfaction with the college environment, a sense of connection to peers and faculty, an increased ability to work as a member of a team, the ability to integrate and apply learning, increased participation in service-learning activities, intellectual growth, and increased use of resources.

FIRST-YEAR SEMINARS, LEARNING COMMUNITIES, AND SERVICE LEARNING

The 2006 survey conducted by the National Resource Center on the First-Year Experience and Students in Transition asked institutions whether their first-year seminars included a service-learning component, and 40 percent responded affirmatively. Some of the campuses profiled by Henscheid (2004) combine LCs, first-year seminars, and service learning. While few studies have sought to determine the effect of adding a service-learning component to LCs, it is clear that service learning has the potential be used as an effective integrating tool, helping students see how the academic content of the LC courses relates to a real-life context, and bringing the LC's theme to life.

Service learning can also serve as a culminating experience for the LC, helping students apply their learning from the LC experience. Eaton, MacGregor, and Schoem (2003) outline the ways that these initiatives can enhance each other. LCs can provide sustained time and space both to conduct the service-learning work and to reflect on that work, and can provide "multiple lenses to examine issues" raised in service learning (4). The researchers note: "Thinking about problems from multiple perspectives can help students develop a more complex understanding" of community problems than they would achieve in a single course focused in one discipline (5). At the same time, service learning brings experiential learning to the LC experience; it focuses students on real, unscripted problems and issues; and it broadens students' thinking about what it means to be a part of a community, expanding that concept beyond the campus. These activities together can help prepare students for life as engaged participants in a diverse democracy.

The campuses profiled in Hesse and Mason's examination of service-learning initiatives that are linked to LCs and first-year seminars conducted assessment of the outcomes related to these linked activities. Faculty could see that in their writing, students made connections "between their lives and the literature, research, and needs of the community" (Hesse and Mason 2003, 13), and that they also "develop[ed] as writers, community members, critical thinkers, and social activists."

Another program focused on the theme of law and diversity and involved a diverse cohort of preprofessional students. These students were kept together for two years and took a full term's worth of classes together each semester while also participating in hands-on work in the community exploring "justice-seeking for those often not well-represented in the legal system" (Eaton 2003, 61). The students were followed when they continued on to law school, where faculty and administrators observed that these particular graduates "contributed productively to discussions of diversity in the law, and assumed leadership positions in their schools" (63). They were found to be more open-minded than their peers, and able to build coalitions across racial groups. They were also committed to pursuing careers in law that would allow them to work for social justice. Eaton (2003) points out that these students came into the experience with interest in this area, so they may have led a life of service with or without the LC experience. But over time, the students continued to talk about the skills they had gained through the LC that enhanced their work in and commitment to the larger community.

Integrating High-Impact Practices

While each of the high-impact practices studied in this literature review show positive outcomes for students, combining multiple approaches may offer even greater potential for student growth and learning. By being intentional about these linkages, colleges and universities can provide more opportunities for students to apply their learning to new contexts and to develop strong communities in and out of the classroom.

CHAPTER 7

Discussion

★ ★ ★ ★ ★ ★ ★ ★ ★ ★ ★ ★ ★ ★ ★ ★

THIS REVIEW SOUGHT TO ANSWER QUESTIONS ABOUT FIVE HIGH-IMPACT PRACTICES: first-year seminars, learning communities, service learning, undergraduate research, and capstone experiences—implemented alone or as part of an integrated effort. We were interested in studying the known outcomes for students who participate in these practices, as well as identifying any differential outcomes for traditionally underserved student populations. We looked for any variables within each practice that increase the likelihood of achieving positive outcomes. And finally, we wanted to assess the quality of the outcomes literature as a whole in order to make future research recommendations.

STUDENT OUTCOMES

Each practice has been labeled as "high impact" in nature (Kuh 2008), and from the research literature it appears clear that each practice does lead to a set of positive outcomes for participants. Across the five practices, the most common outcomes described for student participants include higher grades, higher persistence rates, intellectual gains, greater civic engagement, increased tolerance for and engagement with diversity, and increased interaction with faculty and peers. While the number of studies examining the experiences of students from underserved populations was far more limited, the types of outcomes described for these students included higher grades, higher persistence rates, a greater sense of belonging on campus, and higher rates of graduate school enrollment.

As would be expected, however, the varying effects on the student experience are best examined by looking at each high-impact practice individually. Table 1 describes these known outcomes both for students as a whole and for underserved students in particular.

Table 1

High-Impact Practices: What the Research Shows

FIRST-YEAR SEMINARS

General Effects	Impact on Underserved Students	Moderating Variables	Research Issues
• Higher persistence rates • Higher graduation rates • Short-term positive effect on grade point average • Gains in commitment to social justice/ multicultural awareness • Greater academic and campus engagement • Greater faculty and peer interaction	• Some evidence for short-term increase in grades and persistence rates	• First-year seminar type • Course content • Contact hours	• Predominance of single-institution studies • Variability of first-year seminar formulation/type • Lack of comparison group data • Short-term nature of most research • Outcomes limited to persistence and grades • Examination of outcomes for specific populations rare

CAPSTONE COURSES & PROJECTS

General Effects	Impact on Underserved Students	Moderating Variables	Research Issues
• Limited evidence for applying and integrating knowledge	• Not found	• Time invested • Completion of final product/project • Relationships with faculty/peers	• Lack of empirical studies on outcomes (for any population) • Impact of mediating variables unknown

LEARNING COMMUNITIES

General Effects	Impact on Underserved Students	Moderating Variables	Research Issues
• Higher grades • Higher persistence rates • Ease of college transition • Higher levels of academic engagement • Greater interaction with faculty and peers • Perception of campus as more supportive • Self-report of critical thinking gains • Gains for intellectual development • Higher levels of integrative thinking • Gains in writing and reading skills • Greater appreciation for and engagement with diversity/different viewpoints • Higher rate of civic engagement	• Higher grades • Higher persistence rates • Ease of college transition • Greater interaction with faculty and peers • Helps build identity as learner/ recognize academic potential • Sense of belonging • Gains for intellectual development	• Variability of learning community formulation/type (residential, nonresidential, linked courses, etc.) • Degree of student and faculty interaction • Classroom environment (positive, negative, mixed)	• Predominance of single-institution studies • Variability of learning community formulation/ type • Lack of specificity about learning community elements to make comparisons between formulations • Lack of comparison group data across learning community types • Short-term nature of most research • Reliance on self-reported data • Examination of outcomes for specific populations rare

SERVICE LEARNING

General Effects	Impact on Underserved Students	Moderating Variables	Research Issues
• Higher grades • Higher persistence rates • Academic gains (including application of course learning) • Higher levels of academic engagement • Increases in critical thinking and writing skills • Greater interaction with faculty • Greater levels of civic behavior, social responsibility, understanding of social justice, and sense of self-efficacy • Gains in moral reasoning • Greater tolerance and reduced stereotyping • Greater commitment to service-oriented career	• Increased retention rates • Better academic performance (grades) • Positive changes in civic attitudes • Negative experiences/ isolation due to orientation of service experience	• Characteristics of service experience (type, hours, contact, supervision) • Characteristics of learning experience (reflection, faculty connection of material with service experience)	• Self-selection bias • Short-term nature of most research • Lack of involvement in service-learning experiences by underserved students • Lack of research on experiences of underserved students

UNDERGRADUATE RESEARCH

General Effects	Impact on Underserved Students	Moderating Variables	Research Issues
• Higher rate of persistence • Higher rate of graduate school enrollment • Improvement in research skills • Increased interaction with faculty and peers • Gains in problem solving and critical thinking • Greater satisfaction with educational experience	• Higher rate of persistence • Higher rate of graduate school enrollment • Findings mostly limited to studies of undergraduate research opportunity program/summer research opportunity program students	• Role of faculty mentor • Quality of mentoring relationship	• Lack of empirical studies (vs. program descriptions) • Selection bias (promising students often selected for undergraduate research opportunities) • Unknown impact of mediating variables • Lack of research on outcomes beyond retention and graduate school enrollment

Moderating Variables

For each of the five high-impact practices described in this review, there is tremendous variability in the practice's definition, formulation, and implementation across higher education, even within a single campus. The focus, then, should move toward understanding what, why, and how elements of certain practices have greater benefits for students. A brief list of moderating variables by practice is included in table 1. Across practices, the following elements were identified as potentially having an effect on student outcomes: classroom environment and activities; degree and quality of faculty and student interaction; and number of hours invested (or "time on task"). More research is needed, however, to better understand how these factors affect student learning outcomes, particularly for underserved students. In addition, as described in chapter 6, it is important to consider the potential benefits of integrating two or more high-impact practices into a single effort.

While each practice leads to a range of positive outcomes, these high-impact practices will be most effective when institutions, faculty, and practitioners are intentional in their design and use. While every campus is unique and therefore must design practices with its own goals, culture, and resources in mind, it is important to consider certain elements in that design. The sidebar "Components of Successful High-Impact Practices" converts the list of moderating variables of the four most common practices into a set of recommendations about how to design effective practices.

Research Issues and Recommendations

While most of the high-impact practices described in this review are increasingly found on college campuses, it is only within the last twenty years that they have attained popularity and, as such, have become the subject of systematic evaluation. However, in the course of our review, we found consistent problems in the research related to student outcomes, which means that the evidence for the outcomes described in this review is moderate at best, and very often is weak.

Within each high-impact practice, our research identified components for success. While not exhaustive, the suggestions below detail some best practices for implementing high-impact activities.

1. Expand the focus of such research beyond grades and persistence to include direct measures of student learning outcomes.

2. Intentionally design studies to examine the experiences of underserved students (in some cases this may require over-sampling the particular populations included in this broad category).

3. Design multicourse, multiprogram, and/or multi-institutional studies that examine the use of a practice beyond a single setting.

4. Strive to eliminate the selection bias that occurs when students choose to participate (self-select) in these practices.

5. Utilize comparison groups, with careful attention to their adequacy (e.g., eliminate the usage of comparison groups comprised of students not accepted into a program or course) as well as inclusion of students from underserved populations.

6. Conduct longitudinal research, extending beyond the common time frame of one term or one year beyond participation.

7. Utilize or design measures that provide quantitative and qualitative assessment of student learning, rather than relying solely on self-reported data from students and/or faculty.

Conclusion

High-impact practices have been the subject of much attention and energy in recent years, as have student outcomes as a whole. As we look for ways to demonstrate the positive influence these practices have on our students' learning and development, and look for practices that maximize that influence, the evidence reviewed here makes practices like first-year seminars, learning communities, service learning, undergraduate research, and capstone experiences seem well worth our focus and investment. However, since many of our students do not have the opportunity to participate in even one of these practices during their undergraduate careers, both students and institutions are missing opportunities to experience these powerful benefits. As Behling (2010) wrote, "Our students shouldn't have to rely on luck to have transformative learning experiences, either in the form of the institution they attend, or in the form of the courses they take as they work toward a degree." It is our responsibility to create the "purposeful pathways" that will lead all students to these experiences.

Afterword

★ ★ ★ ★ ★ ★ ★ ★ ★ ★ ★ ★ ★ ★ ★ ★ ★

What's Next? Identifying When High-Impact Practices Are Done Well

ALMA R. CLAYTON-PEDERSEN

SENIOR SCHOLAR, ASSOCIATION OF AMERICAN COLLEGES AND UNIVERSITIES

ASHLEY FINLEY

DIRECTOR OF ASSESSMENT AND RESEARCH, ASSOCIATION OF AMERICAN COLLEGES AND UNIVERSITIES

IN REVIEWING THE EXISTING LITERATURE, Brownell and Swaner have exposed the awesome potential of integrating high-impact practices across the higher education curriculum. These practices are varied enough to fit the spectrum of campus missions, cultures, and needs. Brownell and Swaner have identified a wealth of research pointing to the positive effect of these practices on student learning outcomes. However, closer examination of these practices—both on campuses and within the literature—suggests that what limits their potential isn't a failure of adoption; it's a failure of implementation. Adoption is a necessary but insufficient condition to ensure student success. Brownell and Swaner's work highlights the need for campuses to go beyond simply adopting these practices to carefully considering how to implement them in ways that make their "high impact" a reality.

The limited research on the effects of high-impact practices on the learning outcomes of underserved students underscores two imperatives of implementing these practices effectively. First, the efficacy of high-impact practices means that they must be broadly accessible. The research summarized in this monograph reminds us that an institution can adopt these practices without ensuring that enough or all students benefit from them. Faculty, administrators, and student affairs educators alike need to ask, who is participating in these practices? What should students be getting out of these experiences that will guide their growth and future learning? Institutions must also set clear goals for these practices. Without knowledge of who these practices are reaching and with what success, the potential of high-impact practices will be limited, and it will not be clear how students with a wide array of life experiences, cultural differences, and varied capabilities are or are not benefitting.

Second, access to these practices alone will not ensure that all students benefit. Central to any discussion of high-impact practices is the caveat that they are effective "when done well" (Kuh 2008, 14). Thus, when implementing high-impact practices, the process itself and the quality dimension are critical. For example, identifying the best model of learning communities for a particular campus context is an important element of implementation. But context isn't everything. Institutions must take care to implement models in a way that ensures the students in every learning community have experiences befitting the term "high impact." Doing the latter requires a common set of principles that consider learning objectives that are consistent across the learning communities within a single campus.

Three basic principles can help guide an evaluation of the depth of student experience with all high-impact practices. First, these experiences should *intentionally engage* students. Second, students in these practices should be *engaged in consistent interaction* with peers and faculty, and, perhaps, community members, campus staff, and administrators. Third, these experiences should provide consistent opportunities for *group-based and individual reflection* over time. As the presence and degree of these practices vary, so too will the intensity (and efficacy) of students' experiences and successful attainment of learning outcomes.

INTENTIONALITY

Intentionality requires educators to create coherent learning experiences and to make sure the learning objectives of these experiences are consistently made transparent to students. This means that "a critical component of intentionality involves making sure students know why they are being asked to learn certain outcomes, and reminding faculty who teach to have that discussion with students" (Kean, Mitchell, and Wilson 2008, 6). This intentionality fosters students' ability to integrate and apply knowledge; to recognize the fit between the content, assignments, and activities in the learning experience; to understand what learning outcomes are expected from the engagement; and to connect these outcomes and experiences to the larger goals of the curriculum.

The curriculum and cocurriculum are made intentional when learning

> ➤ is structured appropriately so that students see the connections between their learning within various courses and across individual programs and the overall curriculum, such as general education, the major, and other degree requirements;

> ➤ follows a progression that begins with learners' existing knowledge base and moves them to increasingly more sophisticated levels of learning to better ensure that students can scaffold knowledge to comprehend more advanced concepts;

> ➤ is aligned with program objectives and is designed to meet overall curriculum objectives so that learners can begin to make sense of what may seem like discrete bits of knowledge with no connections among them;

> ➤ is made relevant to students' lives—either by the contemporary or enduring nature of the topic or a student's personal connection with the topic;

> ➤ involves activities in the community that are inclusive and respectful of the community's needs and in which community members as well as faculty members are engaged in facilitating students' achievement of expected learning outcomes.

INTERACTION

Learning does not occur in a vacuum in any learning environment; students interact with faculty, other campus educators, peers, and community members. The research is clear that meaningful interaction between faculty and students plays a large role in students' achievement of learning outcomes (Swaner and Brownell 2008). Moreover, the interactions between students and these various "others" provide a rich source of varied perspectives and contexts for engaged learning. For instance, faculty members socialize students to their discipline as both teachers of content and as mentors. Faculty members are also advisers and critical reviewers of students' work. Students' interactions with campus officials, peers, and community members who are similar and dissimilar to them also help develop their ability to engage diverse perspectives in different contexts. These varied types of interactions contribute to learning when

> ➤ faculty offer mentoring as well as oversight of the learning activities;

> ➤ faculty consider and use students' life experiences to foster deeper engagement in their learning;

- campus officials model respectful engagement with the communities with which students may interact;

- differences between students and those with whom they interact are used to enlarge students' understanding of people from different cultures and backgrounds and to help students respectfully use these differences as learning resources.

REFLECTION

A student's sense of how knowledge relates to life grows when he or she grapples with untidy and unscripted problems (Huber and Hutchings, 2005, iv). Reflection includes "returning to experience; attending to feelings; and evaluating experience" (Jeffs and Smith 1999, 2). However, the most effective structuring of reflection activities occurs once the learning outcomes have been identified, and provides opportunities for reflection components to be incorporated at multiple points in the learning experience—beginning, middle, and end (Gelmon et al. 2001). Additionally, by distributing reflection activities throughout the learning experience, students are afforded their own, self-guided means by which to reach an understanding of the intended learning outcomes (Gelmon et al. 2001). Thus, learning is enhanced through reflection when students

- debate possible solutions to the social challenges presented in the learning experience;

- engage in structured consideration of the course content as it relates to self, others, and the larger society;

- encounter knowledge in new contexts and open-ended, unscripted problems;

- prepare personal writing that requires self-reflection upon a wide variety of subjects, and that situates the self in relation to others;

- are able to combine the new disciplinary/interdisciplinary knowledge gained from the course or program with their existing knowledge, as well as their personal and social experiences; and assess their own knowledge development and knowledge integration in ways that are appropriate for the course, program content, and associated activity.

In the competitive world of higher education, institutions regularly measure success by differentiating the quality of their learning experiences from each other. By doing so, campuses often overlook the research that shows that the greatest source of difference in learning quality tends to be in the learning that happens *within* individual campuses, not between them (see Blaich 2006; National Survey of Student Engagement 2008). Campus leaders at all levels can begin to address this variation by first identifying the principles that define what it means to do high-impact practices "well." Once an institution identifies the characteristics of high-quality, high-impact practices, educators can engage in a rich dialogue about how to gauge who has access to these practices, the integrity of their implementation, and the depth or *intensity* of their implementation. The effect of high-impact practices—especially for underserved students—will be limited if we ignore the *intensity* of the implementation of these practices. The use of these principles can enable educators to assess the implementation process, bring the high-impact practices to scale across educational sectors, and create an "on-ramp" to the next generation of work in closing achievement gaps and reaching essential learning outcomes.

References

Andreasen, R. J., and L. D. Trede. 1998. *A comparison of the perceived benefits of selected activities between capstone and non-capstone courses in a college of agriculture.* Paper presented at the American Vocational Association, New Orleans.

Anselmo, A. 1997. Is there life after freshman seminar? The case for the freshman seminar class reunion. *Journal of the Freshman Year Experience and Students in Transition* 9 (1): 105–130.

Association of American Colleges and Universities. 2007. College learning for the new global century: A report from the National Leadership Council for Liberal Education and America's Promise. Washington, DC: Association of American Colleges and Universities.

Astin, A. W. 1984. Student involvement: A developmental theory for higher education. *Journal of College Student Personnel* 25 (4): 297–308.

Astin, A. W., L. J. Sax, and J. Avalos. 1999. Long-term effects of volunteerism during the undergraduate years. *Review of Higher Education* 22 (2): 187–202.

Astin, A. W., L. J. Vogelgesang, E. K. Ikeda, and J. A. Yee. 2000. *How service learning affects students.* Los Angeles, CA: Higher Education Research Institute.

Avens, C., and R. Zelley. 1992. *QUANTA: An interdisciplinary learning community (Four studies).* Daytona Beach, FL: Daytona Beach Community College.

Balazadeh, N. 1996. Service-learning and the sociological imagination: Approach and assessment. Paper presented at the National Historically Black Colleges and Universities Faculty Development Symposium, Memphis, TN.

Barefoot, B. O. 1992. Helping first-year college students climb the academic ladder: Report of a national survey of freshman seminar programming in American higher education. EdD diss., College of William and Mary.

——. 1993. *Exploring the evidence: Reporting outcomes on freshman seminars.* Columbia, SC: National Resource Center for the Freshman Year Experience.

——. 2000. The first-year experience: Are we making it any better? *About Campus* 4 (6): 12–18.

Barefoot, B. O., C. L. Warnock, M. P. Dickinson, S. E. Richardson, and M. R. Roberts, eds. 1998. *Exploring the evidence: Reporting outcomes of first-year seminars, Volume II.* Columbia, SC: National Resource Center for the First-Year Experience and Students in Transition.

Barrows, S., and M. Goodfellow. 2005. Learning community effects on first-year student success in a general chemistry course. *Journal of the First-Year Experience* 17 (2): 11–22.

Batchelder, T. H., and S. Root. 1994. Effects of an undergraduate program to integrate academic learning and service: Cognitive, prosocial cognitive, and identity outcomes. *Journal of Adolescence* 17 (4): 341–55.

Bauer, K. W., and J. S. Bennett. 2003. Alumni perceptions on the value of undergraduate research. *Journal of Higher Education* 74 (2): 210–230.

Baxter Magolda, M. B. 1992. *Knowing and reasoning in college: Gender-related patterns in students' intellectual development.* San Francisco: Jossey-Bass.

Behling, L. 2010. Changing course. *Liberal education nation: A blog from the LEAP initiative,* January 27. http://blog.aacu.org/index.php/2010/01/27/changing-course/.

Berson, J. S., and W. F. Younkin. 1998. Doing well by doing good: A study of the effects of a service-learning experience on student success. Paper presented at the American Society of Higher Education, Miami, FL.

Blackhurst, A. E., L. D. Akey, and A. J. Bobilya. 2003. A qualitative investigation of student outcomes in a residential learning community. *Journal of the First-Year Experience* 15 (2): 35–59.

Blaich, C. 2006. Critical factors affecting the outcomes of liberal education. Presentation at the Association of American Colleges and Universities General Education Conference, Phoenix, AZ.

Boyer Commission on Educating Undergraduates in the Research University. 1998. *Reinventing undergraduate education: A blueprint for America's research universities.* Stanford, CA: Carnegie Foundation for the Advancement of Teaching.

Boyle-Baise, M., and J. Langford. 2004. There are children here: Service-learning for social justice. *Equity and Excellence in Education* 37 (1): 55–66.

Brower, A. M., and K. M. Dettinger. 1998. What IS a learning community? *About Campus* 3 (5): 15–21.

Brownell, J. E., and L. E. Swaner. 2009. Outcomes of high-impact educational practices: A literature review. *Diversity & Democracy* 12 (2): 4–6.

Clayton-Pedersen, A. R. 2009. Rethinking educational practices to make excellence inclusive. *Diversity & Democracy* 12 (2): 1–3.

Codispoti, F. 2004. A justification of the communitarian model. In *Service-learning: History, theory, and issues,* ed. B.W. Speck and S. L. Hoppe, 99–118. Westport, CT: Praeger.

Council for Opportunity in Education. 2008. What is TRIO? www.coenet.us/ecm/AM/Template. cfm?Section=What_is_TRIO&Template=/CM/HTMLDisplay.cfm&ContentID=7992.

Crews, R. J. 2002. *Higher education service-learning sourcebook.* Westport, CT: Oryx Press.

Einfeld, A., and D. Collins. 2008. The relationships between service-learning, social justice, multicultural competence, and civic engagement. *Journal of College Student Development* 49 (2): 95–109.

Elgren, T., and N. Hensel. 2006. Undergraduate research experiences: Synergies between scholarship and teaching. *Peer Review* 8 (1): 4–7.

Ender, M. G., L. Martin, D. A. Cotter, B. M. Kowaleswski, and J. D. Defiore. 2000. Given an opportunity to reach out: Heterogeneous participation in optional service-learning projects. *Teaching Sociology* 28 (3): 206–19.

Engberg, M. E., and M. J. Mayhew. 2007. The influence of first-year "success" courses on student learning and democratic outcomes. *Journal of College Student Development* 48 (3): 241–258.

Engstrom, C. M., and V. Tinto. 2008a. Access without support is not opportunity. *Change* 40 (1): 46–50.

Engstrom, C. M., and V. Tinto. 2008b. Learning better together: The impact of learning communities on the persistence of low-income students. *Opportunity Matters* 1: 5–21.

Eyler, J., and D. E. Giles, Jr. 1999. *Where's the learning in service-learning?* San Francisco: Jossey-Bass.

Fenzel, L. M. 2005. Multivariate analyses of predictors of heavy episodic drinking and drinking related problems among college students. *Journal of College Student Development* 46 (2): 126–40.

Fidler, P. P. 1991. Relationship of freshman orientation seminars to sophomore return rates. *Journal of the Freshman Year Experience* 3 (1): 7–38.

Fidler, P. P., and M. A. Godwin. 1994. Retaining African-American students through the freshman seminar. *Journal of Developmental Education* 17 (3): 34–40.

Fidler, P. P., and P. S. Moore. 1996. A comparison of effects of campus residence and freshman seminar attendance on freshman dropout rates. *Journal of the Freshman Year Experience and Students in Transition* 8 (2): 7–16.

Foertsch, J., B. B. Alexander, and D. Penberthy. 2000. Summer research opportunity programs (SROPs) for minority undergraduates: A longitudinal study of program outcomes, 1986–1996. *Council on Undergraduate Research Quarterly* 20 (3): 114–119.

Friedman, D. B., and J. S. Alexander. 2007. Investigating a first-year seminar as an anchor course in learning communities. *Journal of the First-Year Experience & Students in Transition* 19 (1): 63–74.

Gardner, J. M., and G. Van der Veer. 1998. The emerging movement to strengthen the senior experience. In *The senior year experience: Facilitating integration, reflection, closure, and transition*, ed. J.N. Gardner, G. Van der Veer, and Associates, 3–20. San Francisco: Jossey-Bass.

Gardner, J. N., G. Van der Veer, and Associates. 1998. *The senior year experience: Facilitating integration, reflection, closure, and transition.* San Francisco: Jossey-Bass.

Gelmon, S. B., B. A. Holland, A. Driscoll, A. Spring, and S. Kerrigan. 2001. *Assessing service-learning and civic engagement: Principles and techniques.* Providence, RI: Campus Compact.

Goodman, K., and E. T. Pascarella. 2006. First-year seminars increase persistence and retention: A summary of the evidence from *How College Affects Students. Peer Review* 8 (3): 26–28.

Gordon, V. 1989. Origins and purposes of the freshman seminar. In *The freshman year experience: Helping students survive and succeed in college*, ed. M. L. Upcraft, J. N. Gardner, and associates, 183–97. San Francisco: Jossey-Bass.

Heinemann, R. L. 1997. The senior capstone, dome or spire? Paper presented at the Annual Meeting of the National Communication Association, Chicago, IL.

Henscheid, J. M. 2000. *Professing the disciplines: An analysis of senior seminars and capstone courses.* Columbia, SC: National Resource Center for the First-Year Experience and Students in Transition.

———. 2004. First-year seminars in learning communities: Two reforms intersect. In *Integrating the first-year experience: The role of learning communities in first-year seminars*, ed. J. M. Henscheid, 1–7. Columbia, SC: National Resource Center for the First-Year Experience and Students in Transition.

Hesse, M. and M. Mason. 2003. Teaching the theme of community. In *Integrating learning communities with service-learning*, ed. J. MacGregor, 9–15. Olympia, WA: The Evergreen State College, Washington Center for Improving the Quality of Undergraduate Education.

Hoppe, S. L. 2004. A synthesis of the theoretical stances. In *Service-learning: History, theory, and issues*, ed. B. W. Speck and S. L. Hoppe, 138–49. Westport, CT: Praeger.

Horn, L., and S. Nevill. 2006. *Profile of undergraduates in U.S. postsecondary education institutions: 2003–04; With a special analysis of community college students.* Washington, DC: National Center for Education Statistics.

Horn, L. J., M. D. Premo, and MPR Associates. 1995. *Profile of undergraduates in U.S. postsecondary education institutions: 1992–1993.* Berkley, CA: MPR Associates.

Hotchkiss, J. L., R. E. Moore, and M. M. Pitts. 2006. Freshman learning communities, college performance, and retention. *Education Economics* 14 (2): 197–210.

House, J. D., and S. J. Kuchynka. 1997. The effects of a freshmen orientation course on the achievement of health science students. *Journal of College Student Development* 38 (5): 540–42.

Hu, S., K. Scheuch, R. Schwartz, J. G. Gayles, and S. Li. 2008. *Reinventing undergraduate education: Engaging college students in research and creative activities.* San Francisco: Jossey-Bass.

Huber, M. T., and P. Hutchings. 2005. *Integrative learning: Mapping the terrain.* Washington, DC: Association of American Colleges and Universities.

Inkelas, K. K., Z. E. Daver, K. E. Vogt, and J. B. Leonard. 2007. Living-learning programs and first-generation college students' academic and social transition to college. *Research in Higher Education* 48 (4): 403–34.

Inkelas, K. K., D. Johnson, Z. Lee., Z, Daver, S. D. Longerbeam, K. Vogt, and J. B. Leonard. 2006. The role of living-learning programs in students' perceptions of intellectual growth at three large universities. *NASPA Journal* 43 (1): 115–43.

Inkelas, K. K., K. E. Vogt, S. D. Longerbeam, J. Owen, and D. Johnson. 2006. Measuring outcomes of living-learning programs: Examining college environments and student learning and development. *The Journal of General Education* 55 (1): 40–76.

Inkelas, K. K., and J. L. Weisman. 2003. Different by design: An examination of student outcomes among participants in three types of living-learning programs. *Journal of College Student Development* 44 (3): 335–368.

Ishiyama, J. 2001. Undergraduate research and the success of first-generation, low-income college students. *Council on Undergraduate Research Quarterly* 22 (1): 36–41.

———. 2007. Expectations and perceptions of undergraduate research mentoring: Comparing first generation, low income White/Caucasian and African American students. *College Student Journal* 41 (3): 540–49.

Jacoby, B. 1996. Service learning in today's higher education. In *Service-learning in higher education: Concepts and practices*, ed. B. Jacoby and Associates, 3–25. San Francisco: Jossey-Bass.

Jaffee, D., A. C. Carle, R. Phillips, and L. Paltoo. 2008. Intended and unintended consequences of first-year learning communities: An initial investigation. *Journal of the First-Year Experience and Students in Transition* 20 (1): 53–70.

James, P. A., P. L. Bruch, and R. R. Jehangir. 2006. Ideas in practice: Building bridges in a multicultural learning community. *Journal of Developmental Education* 29 (3): 10–18.

Jeffs, T., and M. K. Smith. 1999. *Informal education: Conversation, democracy and learning.* 2nd ed. Derbyshire, UK: Education Now.

Jehangir, R. 2008. In their own words: Voices of first-generation college students in a multicultural learning community. *Opportunity Matters* 1: 22–32.

Jessor, R., J. Van Den Bos, J. Vanderryn, F. M. Costa, and M. S. Turbin. 1995. Protective factors in adolescent problem behavior: Moderator effects and developmental change. *Developmental Psychology* 31 (6): 923–33.

Jonides, J. 1995. *Evaluation and dissemination of an undergraduate program to improve retention of at-risk students.* Washington, DC: Fund for the Improvement of Postsecondary Education.

Jonides, J., J. S. Lerner, W. von Hippel, and B. A. Nagda. 1992. Evaluation of minority retention programs: The Undergraduate Research Opportunities Program at the University of Michigan. Paper presented at the Annual Meeting of the American Psychological Association, Washington, DC.

Karukstis, K. K., and T. E. Elgren, eds. 2007. *Developing and sustaining a research-supportive curriculum: A compendium of successful practices.* Washington, DC: Council on Undergraduate Research.

Kaufman, L., and J. Stocks, eds. 2004. *Reinvigorating the undergraduate experience: Successful models supported by NSF's AIRE/RAIRE Program.* Washington, DC: Council on Undergraduate Research.

Kean, R. C., N. D. Mitchell, and D. E. Wilson. 2008. Toward intentionality and transparency: Analysis and reflection on the process of general education reform. *Peer Review* 10 (4): 4–8.

Keup, J. R., and B. O. Barefoot. 2005. Learning how to be a successful student: Exploring the impact of first-year seminars on student outcomes. *Journal of the First-Year Experience* 17 (1): 11–47.

King, P. M., and K. S. Kitchener. 1994. *Developing reflective judgment: Understanding and promoting intellectual growth and critical thinking in adolescents and adults.* San Francisco: Jossey-Bass.

Kinkead, J. 2005. Learning through inquiry: An overview of undergraduate research. In *Valuing and supporting undergraduate research*, ed. J. Kinkead, 5–18. San Francisco: Jossey-Bass.

Knefelkamp, L. 1974. Developmental instruction: Fostering intellectual and personal growth in college students. PhD diss., Univ. of Minnesota.

Kuh, G. D. 2008. *High-impact educational practices: What they are, who has access to them, and why they matter.* Washington, DC: Association of American Colleges and Universities.

Kuh, G. D., J. Kinzie, J. A. Buckley, B. K. Bridges, and J. C. Hayek. 2007. *Piecing together the student success puzzle: Research, propositions, and recommendations.* San Francisco: Jossey-Bass.

Kuh, G. D., J. Kinzie, J. H. Schuh, E. J. Whitt, and Associates. 2005. *Student success in college: Creating conditions that matter.* San Francisco: Jossey-Bass.

Kuh, G. D., J. H. Schuh, and E. J. Whitt. 1991. *Involving colleges: Successful approaches to fostering student learning and development outside the classroom.* San Francisco: Jossey-Bass.

Lang, D. J. 2007. The impact of a first-year experience course on the academic performance, persistence, and graduation rates of first-semester college students at a public research university. *Journal of the First-Year Experience and Students in Transition* 19 (1): 9–25.

Lee, V. S., ed. 2004. *Teaching and learning through inquiry: A guidebook for institutions and instructors.* Sterling, VA: Stylus.

Leskes, A., and R. Miller. 2006. *Purposeful pathways: Helping students achieve key learning outcomes.* Washington, DC: Association of American Colleges and Universities.

Levine, A. 1998. A president's personal and historical perspective. In *The senior year experience: Facilitating integration, reflection, closure, and transition*, ed. J. N. Gardner, G. Van der Veer, and Associates, 51–59. San Francisco: Jossey-Bass.

Lichtenstein, M. 2005. The importance of classroom environments in the assessment of learning community outcomes. *Journal of College Student Development* 46 (4): 341–56.

Longerbeam, S. D., and W. E. Sedlacek. 2006. Attitudes toward diversity and living-learning outcomes among first- and second-year college students. *NASPA Journal* 43 (1): 40–55.

Lopatto, D. 2004. Survey of Undergraduate Research Experiences (SURE): First findings. *Cell Biology Education* 3 (4): 270–77.

———. 2006. Undergraduate research as a catalyst for liberal learning. *Peer Review* 8 (1): 22–25.

Mabry, J. B. 1998. Pedagogical variations in service-learning and student outcomes: How time, contact and reflection matter. *Michigan Journal of Community* Service 5: 32-47.

Madden, S. J., ed. 2000. *Service learning across the curriculum: Case applications in higher education*. Lanham, MD: University Press of America.

Maisto, A. A., and M. W. Tammi. 1991. The effect of a content-based freshman seminar on academic and social integration. *Journal of the Freshman Year Experience* 3 (2): 29–47.

Merkel, C. A. 2001. *Undergraduate research at six research universities: A pilot study for the Association of American Universities*. Washington, DC.: Association of American Universities.

McCormick, A. C, J. V. Moore III, and G. D. Kuh. 2010. Working in college: Its relationship to student engagement and educational outcomes. In *Understanding the working college student: Implications for policy, administrators, academic affairs, and institutional support*, ed. L. W. Perna. Sterling, VA: Stylus.

Miller, J. W., J. C. Janz, and C. Chen. 2007. The retention impact of a first-year seminar on students with varying pre-college academic performance. *Journal of the First-Year Experience and Students in Transition* 19 (1): 47–62.

Mueller, K. 1961. *Student personnel work in higher education*. Boston: Houghton Mifflin.

Myers-Lipton, S. J. 1998. Effect of a comprehensive service-learning program on college students' civic responsibility. *Teaching Sociology* 26 (4): 243–58.

———. 2002. Service-learning and success in sociology. In *Included in sociology: Learning climates that cultivate racial and ethnic diversity*, ed. J. Chin, C. W. Berheide, and D. Rome, 202–18. Washington, DC.: American Association for Higher Education and American Sociological Association.

Nagda, B. A., S. R. Gregerman, J. Jonides, W. von Hippel, and J. S. Lerner. 1998. Undergraduate student-faculty research partnerships affect student retention. *The Review of Higher Education* 22 (1): 55–72.

National Resource Center on the First-Year Experience and Students in Transition. 2006. *Preliminary summary of results from the 2006 National Survey on First-Year Seminars*. Columbia, SC: National Resource Center on the First-Year Experience and Students in Transition.

National Survey of Student Engagement. 2007. *Experiences that matter: Enhancing student learning and success*. Bloomington, IN: Indiana University Center for Postsecondary Research.

———. 2008. *Promoting engagement for all students: The imperative to look within*. Bloomington, IN: Indiana University Center for Postsecondary Research.

——. 2009. *Assessment for improvement: Tracking student engagement over time.* Bloomington, IN: Indiana University Center for Postsecondary Research.

Pascarella, E. T., T. A. Seifert, and C. E. Blaich. 2010. How effective are the NSSE benchmarks in predicting important educational outcomes? *Change* 42 (1):16–22.

Pascarella, E. T., and P. T. Terenzini. 1991. *How college affects students: Findings and insights from twenty years of research.* San Francisco: Jossey-Bass.

——. 2005. *How college affects students: A third decade of research*, vol. 2. San Francisco: Jossey-Bass.

Pascarella, E. T., P. T. Terenzini, and G. S. Bliming. 1994. The impact of residential life on students. In *Realizing the educational potential of residence halls*, ed. C. C. Schroeder, P. Mable, and Associates, 22–52. San Francisco: Jossey-Bass.

Perry, W. G. 1970. *Forms of intellectual and ethical development in the college years: A scheme.* New York: Holt, Rinehart, and Winston.

Pickron-Davis, M. C. 1999. Black students in community service-learning: Critical reflections about self and identity. PhD diss., Univ. of Pennsylvania.

Pike, G. R. 2002. The differential effects of on- and off-campus living arrangements on students' openness to diversity. *NASPA Journal* 39 (4): 283–99.

Pike, G. R., C. C. Schroeder, and T. R. Berry. 1997. Enhancing the educational impact of residence halls: The relationship between residential learning communities and first-year college experiences and persistence. *Journal of College Student Development* 38 (6): 609–21.

Policy Center on the First Year of College. 2002. Second national survey of first-year academic practices. www.jngi.org/2002nationalsurvey.

Porter, S. R., and R. L. Swing. 2006. Understanding how first-year seminars affect persistence. *Research in Higher Education* 47 (1): 89–109.

The Regents of the University of California at Berkeley. 2008. *UC Berkeley accreditation*: Preparing students for successful capstone experiences. http://vpapf.chance.berkeley.edu/accreditation/ee_essays_1.html.

Roldan, M., A. Strage, and D. David. 2004. A framework for assessing academic service-learning across disciplines. In *New perspectives in service-learning: Research to advance the field*, ed. M. Welch and S. H. Billig, 39–59. Greenwich, CT: Information Age Publishing.

Roose, D., J. Daphne, A. G. Miller, W. Norris, R. Peacock, C. White, and G. White. 1997. *Black student retention study*: Oberlin College. Oberlin, OH: Oberlin College.

Rowan-Kenyon, H., M. Soldner, and K. K. Inkelas. 2007. The contributions of living-learning programs on developing sense of civic engagement in undergraduate students. *NASPA Journal* 44 (4): 750–78.

Russell, S. H., M. P. Hancock, and J. McCullough. 2007. Benefits of undergraduate research experiences. *Science* 316 (5824): 548–49.

Schnell, C. A., K. S. Louis, and C. Doetkott. 2003. The first-year seminar as a means of improving college graduation rates. *Journal of the First-Year Experience* 15 (1): 53–76.

Schussler, D. L., and E. G. Fierros. 2008. Students' perceptions of their academics, relationships, and sense of belonging: Comparisons across residential learning communities. *Journal of the First-Year Experience and Students in Transition* 20 (1): 71–96.

Schwitzer, A. M., T. V. McGovern, and S. B. Robbins. 1991. Adjustment outcomes of a freshman seminar: A utilization-focused approach. *Journal of College Student Development* 32 (6): 484–489.

Scrivener, S., D. Bloom, A. LeBlanc, C. Paxson, C. E. Rouse, and C. Sommo. 2008. *A good start: Two-year effects of a freshman learning community program at Kingsborough Community College.* New York: MDRC.

Seymour, E., A. B. Hunter, S. L. Laursen, and T. Deantoni. 2004. Establishing the benefits of research experiences in the sciences: First findings from a three-year study. *Science Education* 88 (4): 493–594.

Seifert, T. A., E. T. Pascarella, K. M. Goodman, M. H. Salisbury, and C. E. Blaich. 2010. Liberal arts colleges and good practices in undergraduate education: Additional evidence. *Journal of College Student Development* 51 (1): 1–22.

Shulman, L.S. 2002. Making differences: A table of learning. *Change* 34 (6): 36–44.

Smedick, W. D. 1996. A study of the effects of a volunteer service program at an urban-based institution of higher education on the current level of service achieved by alumni who had participated in the program. PhD diss., Morgan State University.

Sommers, B. J. 1997. The freshman year experience and geography: Linking student retention and the introductory geography curriculum. *Journal of Geography* 96 (5): 243–249.

Stanton, T. K., D. E. Giles Jr., and N. I. Cruz. 1999. *Service learning: A movement's pioneers reflect on its origins, practice, and future.* San Francisco: Jossey-Bass.

Starke, M. C., M. Harth, and F. Sirianni. 2001. Retention, bonding, and academic achievement: Success of a first-year seminar. *Journal of the First-Year Experience* 13 (2): 7–35.

Stephen, J., D. H. Parente, and R. C. Brown. 2002. Seeing the forest and the trees: Balancing functional and integrative knowledge using large-scale simulations in capstone business strategy classes. *Journal of Management Education* 26 (2): 164–93.

Swaner, L. and J. Brownell. 2008. *Outcomes of high-impact practices for underserved students: A review of the literature.* Washington, DC: Association of American Colleges and Universities.

Swing, R. L. 2002. *How many weekly contact hours is enough?* www.sc.edu/fye/resources/assessment/essays/swing-8.28.02_pdfs/hours.pdf.

——. 2004. The improved learning outcomes of linked versus stand-alone first-year seminars. In *Integrating the first-year experience: The role of learning communities in first-year seminars,* ed. J. M. Henscheid, 9-15. Columbia, SC: National Resource Center for the First-Year Experience and Students in Transition.

Tartter, V. C. 1996. *City College report to FIPSE.* New York: City College Research Foundation.

Taylor, K., and Associates. 2003. *Learning community research and assessment: What we know now.* Olympia, WA: Washington Center for Improving the Quality of Undergraduate Education.

Tinto, V. 1993. *Leaving college: Rethinking the causes and cures of student attrition.* 2nd ed. Chicago: The University of Chicago Press.

———. 1997. Classrooms as communities: Exploring the educational character of student persistence. *Journal of Higher Education* 68 (6): 599–623.

Tinto, V., and A. Goodsell. 1993. A longitudinal study of freshman interest groups at the University of Washington. Washington, DC: Office of Educational Research and Improvement.

Tinto, V., and A. G. Love. 1995. *A longitudinal study of learning communities at La Guardia Community College.* Washington, DC: Office of Educational Research and Improvement.

Tobolowsky, B. F., B. E. Cox, and M. T. Wagner, eds. 2005. *Exploring the evidence: Reporting the research on first-year seminars.* Columbia, SC: National Resource Center for the First-Year Experience and Students in Transition.

Upcraft, M. L., J. N. Gardner, and B. O. Barefoot. 2005. *Challenging and supporting the first-year student: A handbook for improving the first year of college.* San Francisco: Jossey-Bass.

Vogelgesang, L. J., and A. W. Astin. 2000. Comparing the Effects of Community Service and Service-Learning. *Michigan Journal of Community Service Learning* 7: 25–34.

Waldron, V. R., and S. C. Yungbluth. 2007. Assessing student outcomes in communication-intensive learning communities: A two-year longitudinal study of academic performance and retention. *Southern Communication Journal* 72 (3): 285–302.

Wechsler, H., G. W. Dowdall, A. Davenport, and S. Castillo. 1995. Correlates of college student binge drinking. American Journal of Public Health 85 (7): 921–26.

Widick, C. 1975. An evaluation of developmental instruction in a university setting. PhD diss., Univ. of Minnesota.

Wilkie, C., and S. Kuckuck. 1989. A longitudinal study of the effects of a freshman seminar. *Journal of the Freshman Year Experience* 1 (1): 7–16.

Williford, A. M., L. Chapman, and T. Kahrig. 2000-2001. The university experience course: A longitudinal study of student performance, retention, and graduation. *Journal of College Student Retention* 2 (4): 327–40.

Zawacki, K. G. 1997. Personal and family factors related to service learning in an undergraduate course on diversity. PhD diss., Michigan State Univ.

Zhao, C., and G. D. Kuh. 2004. Adding value: Learning communities and student engagement. *Research in Higher Education* 45 (2): 115–38.

Zheng, J. L., K. P. Saunders, M. C. Shelley III, and D. F. Whalen. 2002. Predictors of academic success for freshmen residence hall students. *Journal of College Student Development* 43 (2): 267–83.

Zlotkowski, E. 1999. Pedagogy and engagement. In *Colleges and universities as citizens,* ed. R. G. Bringle, R. Games, and E. A. Malloy, 96–120. Needham Heights, MA: Allyn and Bacon.

About the Authors

★ ★ ★ ★ ★ ★ ★ ★ ★ ★ ★ ★ ★ ★ ★

JAYNE E. BROWNELL is assistant vice president for student affairs at Hofstra University, where, among other responsibilities, she leads the planning and assessment efforts of the Division of Student Affairs. Before arriving at Hofstra in 2006, Brownell worked at the University of Michigan, Columbia University, and Vassar College. She has spent more than fifteen years working in academic advising, residence life, and student activities. She earned her MA, EdM, and EdD in higher education/student personnel administration from Teachers College, Columbia University.

LYNN E. SWANER has served in various capacities in higher education, including a graduate faculty member at the School of Education, Long Island University C.W. Post Campus; national grant evaluator for the Bringing Theory to Practice project of the Association of American Colleges and Universities; and academic and student affairs administrator at Columbia University and Long Island University C.W. Post Campus. Swaner holds an EdD in higher education from Teachers College, Columbia University, and an MS in counseling from Long Island University C.W. Post Campus, as well as Licensed Mental Health Counselor, National Certified Counselor, and Approved Clinical Supervisor credentials. Currently, Swaner consults with educational institutions and organizations in the areas of teaching and learning, faculty development, and accreditation.